ASSERTIVENESS:
A PRACTICAL APPROACH

DEDICATION

To those we love

ASSERTIVENESS:
A PRACTICAL APPROACH

STEPHANIE HOLLAND
& CLARE WARD

Speechmark Publishing Ltd
Telford Road • Bicester • Oxon OX26 4LQ • UK

Published by
Speechmark Publishing Ltd, Telford Road, Bicester, Oxon OX26 4LQ, United Kingdom
Telephone: +44 (0) 1869 244 644   Fax: +44 (0) 1869 320 040
www.speechmark.net

© S Holland & C Ward, 1990

Reprinted 1991, 1992, 1993, 1994, 1995, 1997, 1998, 1999, 2000, 2002, 2003, 2005

Illustrations & cover by Tracy Whitbread

002-0855/Printed in Great Britain/1010

British Library Cataloguing in Publication Data
Holland, Stephanie
    Assertiveness : a practical approach
    1. Assertiveness (Psychology)
    I. Title   II. Ward, Clare
    302.2

    ISBN 0 86388 379 6
    (Previously published by Winslow Press under ISBN 0 86388 081 9)

Contents

Foreword

As the popularity of assertiveness training has spread, many health professionals have approached me wanting to know how to teach assertive skills to their own client groups. How could the basic programme be adapted? Could the skills be taught to those who were very anxious or depressed? Were the skills relevant to those with special needs or difficulties? Could you run a group within a hospital or should you teach on an individual basis?

These questions — and many others related to them — are comprehensively answered in this welcome book by Stephanie Holland and Clare Ward. They have combined their clinical experience and their enthusiasm for assertiveness training to produce a carefully thought-out, clear guide to the teaching of this subject in a specialised context.

The detailed exposition of the content of the programme is studded with examples and illustrations which help root the concepts in everyday reality. This is followed by an admirably practical step-by-step guide to running a group, including suggestions as to the choice of venue, time-structure, detailed session plans, exercises and group activities appropriate to each stage of the training programme. The book's straightforward, simple style will make it invaluable for those wishing to teach assertive skills as part of their work in mental health or allied therapeutic fields.

When I started teaching this subject in 1977, it was my specific goal to lessen the clinical emphasis of assertiveness training and to establish it firmly within an educational context. With the publication of this book, the wheel appears to have come full circle. For this reason I was especially pleased to note the tone of the authors' recommendations to their readers. They encourage would-be facilitators to learn the skills first-hand by attending a class themselves; they stress the notion of equality even within a clinical setting by suggesting that facilitators view the teaching of assertiveness as more a process of sharing with others their own learning, mistakes, difficulties and triumphs than the more conventional manner of teaching from a standpoint of distance and expertise.

I am excited at the prospect of these seeds finding fertile ground.

ANNE DICKSON

About Ourselves

Stephanie Holland is a speech therapist with 12 years' experience of working with a wide variety of communication disorders. She recently left the National Health Service to work as a freelance trainer in order to achieve her ambition of fostering growth in herself, the people she trains and most importantly her half-acre vegetable garden!

Clare Ward is an occupational therapist specialising in the field of mental health. She presently works in a Counselling and Psychotherapy Unit and, on a part-time basis, offers freelance training to a variety of organisations. Her independence, her great zest for life and her total commitment to the concept of personal growth are the qualities she most values in herself.

In 1987 Clare and Stephanie trained with Anne Dickson as assertiveness trainers, and became members of the Redwood Women's Training Association.

Preface

The idea of writing this book evolved from a strong desire to share with others the enormous gains we have derived from our involvement with assertiveness. Learning to communicate assertively has had a dramatic impact on both our lives. Right from the beginning of our assertiveness training we were aware of how enormously valuable this material could be in helping our clients. Many people come to us with poor communication skills and an extremely low level of self-esteem. Here was a method of treatment which could tackle both areas simultaneously.

We feel that this book is significantly enhanced by the combination of skills from our different types of professional training. We do not claim to have all the answers, since the learning process is ongoing, but our experiences over the last few years have shown how powerful this material is, and in writing this book we are hoping to share some of our skills and enthusiasm.

This book offers an opportunity for professionals from all backgrounds to develop an improved understanding of assertiveness training, and to have at hand a working manual from which they can apply the principles of assertiveness both to themselves and to their clients.

There is a growing awareness of the relevance of assertiveness training amongst our colleagues, as is borne out by our own experiences in working with a wide variety of staff and client groups. Our aims in producing this book are

▶ to demonstrate assertiveness as a valid communication skill, relevant to trainer and trainee alike;

▶ to encourage the use of assertiveness training within the caring professions;

▶ to demonstrate that the principles of assertiveness are applicable to a wide variety of client groups;

▶ to provide a practical programme which can be adapted for use at any level.

Our experience of using assertiveness as a form of therapy has been mainly with the following groups: people with learning difficulties; people who feel depressed and anxious; people who stammer; and people with problem eating patterns. This list reflects our own clinical specialities but the reader may wish to use assertiveness with other groups or individuals. Our advice would be to try it, as we believe the material is relevant to most of our clients, regardless of the nature of their problem.

Although the aim of this book is to encourage you to use the material with your clients, we hope that you will be inspired to apply the principles of assertiveness to your own lives.

STEPHANIE HOLLAND
CLARE WARD
August 1990

Acknowledgements

Our thanks go to Catherine McAllister of Winslow Press for giving us the opportunity to write this book; to Celia Levy for her time and advice; to Viv Whittaker for the loan of her remote hideaway in Wensleydale; to Tracy Whitbread for all her hard work in designing the excellent graphics; and to Wendy Lawson, for her last-minute rescue operation!

This book would have been impossible to produce without the invaluable help of our partners, David and Richard. The endless hours they spent battling with the word processor, their perceptive comments on the text and the constant supply of bramble tea have all been essential to the making of this book. Their unfailing love and support and total commitment to the principles of assertiveness have inspired us throughout. To them both we return our love and gratitude.

In writing this book we have to acknowledge the debt of gratitude we owe to Anne Dickson from whose writing and training materials we gained our inspiration.

Introduction

We would like to stress the importance of reading the whole of this book, working through each chapter before embarking on any of the exercises suggested in Appendix I, or attempting to use the material as a treatment method. The idea of the book is to provide readers with all the information they need to use assertiveness as a form of therapy, either with individuals or groups. Those with experience of psychotherapy or counselling may find the material echoes much of the philosophy of such an approach. However we have written *Assertiveness: A Practical Approach* with the intention of encouraging clinicians from all backgrounds to adopt assertiveness as part of their treatment programmes, and therefore have attempted to provide as much practical information as possible.

The order in which we have presented the material is the one which we suggest you follow. It is vital, for example, that people have a clear understanding of behaviour types, the skills of assertiveness and their rights before they attempt to say 'No', or confront someone else's behaviour. Each chapter is devoted to a particular aspect of assertiveness and contains all the basic information you need for each session.

In Chapter 11 we discuss the application of assertiveness as a form of treatment based on our own experiences with different client groups. Appendix I is divided into ten sections, which correspond to the relevant chapters. Each section contains an outline session plan, which is based on a two-hour group session. We recognise that not everyone will work in this way: some therapists may only have half an hour with an individual, or an hour-long group. The purpose of this plan is to provide you with a flexible programme which can be adapted to suit the needs of your clients. We have included handouts which summarise the main points from each chapter and which can be used both as a reminder for the client and as a teaching aid for the therapist. You will also find examples of exercises which can be used in each session.

It is useful at this stage to consider the techniques that we use during the course, as we will be making reference to them throughout the book. We find it helpful to follow the same format for every session: Opening exercise, sharing and feedback; Facilitator's input and discussion; Role-play and feedback; Closing exercise.

Opening exercise — the way we start every session is to ask people to share one positive and one negative experience, and to identify what this has taught them about themselves. This exercise is described in more detail in *Appendix I*.

Feedback — encouraging people to share their thoughts and feelings helps them to identify with others and builds up trust in the group. The most appropriate times to encourage feedback are after small-group work and role-play.

Facilitator's input — the content for each session has been detailed in the corresponding chapter and the handouts provide a concise account of the main points to emphasise. Be aware of the need to encourage discussion rather than lecturing to the group. A useful way of doing this is to use the technique of 'brainstorming' which encourages the spontaneous free flowing of ideas from all members of the group. The ideas need to be recorded as they are given, however bizarre or unusual they may seem. There are no right or wrong answers: each person's contribution is valid.

Role-play — the skills of assertiveness are taught through the medium of role-play, where we concentrate upon our behaviour and its effect on others. Role-play is an absolutely essential part of any course. We have never known anyone, ourselves included, who has not expressed some anxiety about participating in role-play, especially if they think they are always going to have to do so in front of a large group. To allay these fears it is important to give the group the opportunity to share anxieties from the beginning of any course, and for the therapist to explain right from the start *what role-play is about*. People often think that role-play is a form of theatre, but we are not acting; instead we are reliving a situation and trying out new ways of dealing with a problem within a safe environment. In doing so, we will experience some of the feelings which would be generated in the real-life situation. Receiving feedback through others' observation of our role-play helps us to learn the effect our behaviour has on others, and how we could deal with the situation more assertively.

Closing exercise — the way we close each group is to ask people to share something that is personal to them, which relates to the content of the session. Examples of this are given in Appendix I. As facilitators, we always join in both the opening and closing exercises, sharing our own experiences and feelings. This is a really positive way of modelling equality within the group, and demonstrates that our own learning is continuous.

1 Introduction to Assertiveness

Assertiveness and You

Assertiveness training looks deceptively easy. To put it simply, it is a form of behaviour therapy with an extremely powerful message, which needs to be handled with respect. There is a growing awareness amongst health professionals of the value of using counselling and psychotherapy techniques, both in a professional and a personal context. Assertiveness is directly linked with this area of personal growth and development.

We believe that reading this book can never be a substitute for attending a course for yourself. Assertiveness training is, for the most part, experiential and we therefore strongly recommend that you experience it for yourself at first hand. With this in mind we have listed various training opportunities in Appendix II. The advantages in attending a course for yourself include better communication, the reduction of stress through the ability to set clear limits and the honest expression of feelings. These are valuable skills to learn; you and your clients can only benefit as a result.

Change

Training in assertiveness demonstrates to us that we are all capable of change. Altering behaviour patterns that we have lived with for many years can, on the one hand, be exciting and stimulating, but on the other it can be understandably scary. Assertiveness is concerned with making choices, and therefore it is important that individuals choose for themselves whether they wish to make these changes or not. They need to understand just what is entailed and be reassured that any changes they make will be gradual and supported. We are creatures of habit and familiarity is often the safest route to take. Relationships are complex to say the least, and when one partner begins to assert themselves, the other is likely to feel threatened and may resist the change. This is another important point to be discussed with your clients, so that they are aware of the potential effects that the training can have on their lives. We always suggest that they talk with those around them about the changes they are attempting to make in themselves, as this can help to avoid any resentment and misunderstanding.

This was demonstrated when Tony's new-found confidence and increased fluency led him to reclaim some of the tasks that, as a stammerer, he had previously left to his wife, such as ordering food in a restaurant and complaining if the service was poor. In the group, he shared his confusion about his wife's lack of enthusiasm for his assertive behaviour, and as a result realised how his changes were affecting her. This helped him to empathise with her feelings of resentment caused by the reversal of their roles. When he arrived home that night he was able to share his feelings with her, as a step towards resolving the problem.

Personal Change

We are often tempted to try to change other people's behaviour, rather than our own: "She'd be a much better person if she went on the course I suggested"; "I've told him not to drink so much, he'd be a lot happier if he didn't." Trying to change another person is ultimately an aggressive act, an attempt to impose our will on someone else, regardless of their wishes. The reality is that we can only ever change ourselves. However, when we do so, other people are often enabled to make their own changes.

Defining Assertiveness

There are many definitions of assertiveness. We list here the ones we consider to be the most important:

▶ The ability to express our ideas and feelings, both positive and negative, in an open, direct and honest manner;
▶ The ability to stand up for our rights while respecting the rights of others;
▶ The ability to take responsibility for ourselves and our actions without judging or blaming other people;
▶ The ability to find a compromise where conflict exists.

Before presenting these ideas to your clients it is useful to ask them how they perceive assertiveness. Responses we have received which reflect commonly held misconceptions include: "It's about learning to get my own way"; "It means I'll be able to win all my arguments"; "It's standing up for my rights and to hell with the rest of them"; "Assertiveness is about manipulating people without them noticing." In fact all these definitions describe aggressive rather than assertive behaviour and it is very important that this misunderstanding be clarified at the beginning of any course.

The first session provides such an opportunity. It is also important to make time for people to get to know each other and share their expectations about the course. One of the first exercises is that of establishing the group 'rules'. Confidentiality is the most important, as people need this in order to feel safe enough to share their experiences.

If people wish to develop their understanding of assertiveness they can easily do this by reading some of the books listed in the appendix. Assertive behaviour, as contrasted with aggression or passivity, is discussed in more detail in the next chapter.

2 Behaviour Types

Introduction

There are basically four different types of behaviour: *passivity*, *direct aggression*, *indirect aggression* and *assertion*. Nobody is completely aggressive, passive or assertive all the time. It is important to appreciate that none of these behaviours are wholly right or wrong; they are just different and have different effects and consequences.

Learning to Accept our Behaviour

Each one of us has learnt to behave aggressively, indirectly, passively and assertively in different situations throughout our lives. Although there can be a temptation to identify with one particular type of behaviour it is important to acknowledge the wide variety of our responses. People are sometimes surprised; they often come on a course, with the idea that they are totally passive or aggressive, denying the fact that they also act assertively on many occasions. It can be helpful to present the different behaviour types in the form of caricatures, such as those in this chapter's handout. This can help people to identify with each behaviour type. Making it amusing means that it becomes less threatening. We need to be able to accept the behaviour that we are trying to change; we cannot change something in ourselves if we do not even acknowledge that it exists. Making the distinction between these different behaviours means looking at them in more depth.

Passivity

This is the 'doormat' syndrome, where we allow ourselves to be trampled on by other people. It is characterised by a feeling of powerlessness and an inability to take control of our lives. Our self-esteem is very low, tentatively bolstered by pleasing other people and giving them what they want, regardless of our own needs. This overriding need to please and placate those around us results in our having difficulty in standing up for our rights or making clear decisions. The victim in us feels that life has handed us a raw deal and, as a consequence, we have a tendency to avoid taking any responsibility for our own feelings or actions. No matter how people try to help us, we respond with resistance: change is too risky and painful. If confronted or threatened we usually give in or run away. The effect of this on other people is often sheer frustration, which is what Alan felt whenever Kay showed her passive side.

> When Alan asked Kay where she wanted to go on holiday this summer, she shrugged her shoulders and replied, "I don't mind dear, why don't you choose?"
>
> Alan suggested that they tried going abroad for a change.
>
> "Well, if that's what you want, it's OK with me."
>
> Alan felt his irritation grow as he attempted to encourage her, just for once, to offer an opinion. "For God's sake Kay, tell me what you really want!"
>
> Kay looked hurt. "But I've told you, I'm quite happy with whatever you decide. You are always moaning at me, when all I'm trying to do is please you."
>
> In the silence that followed, they both felt upset and frustrated, and were still no nearer to deciding where to spend their holiday.

Direct Aggression

This type of behaviour stems from an intrinsic desire to win at all costs, and it is often confused with assertion. It is true that, when we behave aggressively, we stand up for our rights, express our views and state our needs, but the one important difference is that we do this without any thought or consideration for others' feelings. Compromise is impossible because it may mean 'losing'. If threatened or challenged we attack; the attack may be verbal or physical, and others' response to it is either to back off, become defensive, or to respond with similar force. People often mistake aggressive behaviour for a manifestation of supreme confidence. In fact our self-esteem is often extremely low, and our means of building it up is to put others down, thus chalking up yet another victory for ourselves.

> June sometimes used aggression as a way of boosting her poor self-confidence. She walked into the canteen for lunch, feeling rotten because her boss had criticised her work earlier in the day. She ordered her food abruptly, and the assistant, who was new that day, made a mistake, giving her the wrong order.
>
> "You stupid girl, this isn't what I asked for; can't you do your job properly?"
>
> The assistant apologised profusely for her mistake, offering to change the order.
>
> "Oh don't bother, I'm late enough as it is." The assistant was left feeling bewildered and hurt as June stormed off to eat her meal, failing to recognise the real reason for her aggressive outburst.

Indirect Aggression

This behaviour often results from the fear which exists within our culture of being openly aggressive. Indirect aggression is often seen as the softer option, but in fact its effect can be just as devastating, involving the manipulation of others, through guilt and emotional blackmail. Whereas being the victim of open aggression can be likened to being attacked by a bulldozer, suffering indirect aggression is like being fired at by a sniper: the weapon hits home just as hard, but there is no trace of the attacker. It is harder to identify this type of aggression, because of its subtlety; it is also more difficult to challenge: when it is confronted, there is always denial. Never risking a direct expression of our thoughts and feelings, we create instead an undercurrent of guilty unease, the aim of which is to manipulate others into doing what we want. Responses to this vary from bewilderment to frustration. As with open aggression, our self-esteem is low, boosted by the success of our manipulation and the avoidance of any direct expression of our feelings. It can be very difficult to acknowledge when we are being indirectly aggressive, as was the case with John.

> John and Brian worked together on the same project and, on the face of it, seemed to get on very well. John never openly challenged Brian's work but sometimes used a stream of sarcastic jokes and put-downs instead.
>
> "Watching you work is like watching paint dry; do you think you could actually move into second gear for a change?"
>
> Normally Brian would have laughed weakly, but inside he felt hurt and this time he tried to challenge John.
>
> "I'm fed up with all these comments about my work; I wish you'd give it a rest."
>
> John looked affronted. "Don't get so worked up old man; can't you take a joke?"
>
> Brian felt guilty but he was not sure why; perhaps John was only joking after all. As John walked away he shook his head, thinking about how sensitive some people were, completely failing to recognise his own indirect aggression.

Assertion

The key to assertive behaviour is feeling good about ourselves. It means taking responsibility for our thoughts, feelings and actions, instead of blaming or judging others. Standing up for our rights and expressing our needs is done with consideration for the other person's rights and needs, resulting in equal communication. This approach shuns the win/lose idea, and works instead towards a situation of mutual compromise, where both parties feel acknowledged. As our self-esteem is high, we are more able to admit to our faults and mistakes without feeling totally devastated. Confrontation and criticism can be handled honestly without resorting to defensiveness. We can allow ourselves to take risks and make choices based on our own feelings and needs.

Assertion means feeling on an equal level with others, whoever they may be, and being honest about our feelings, expressing them openly and clearly. Assertive behaviour involves taking the initiative, rather than waiting for something to happen. This results in a feeling of inner strength and enables us to take control of our lives.

> Tilly was unhappy with the steak she had been served in the restaurant. "This steak is rare and I asked for medium; I'd like it changed, please."
>
> The waiter looked harassed. "I'm very sorry Madam, we have been so busy tonight, I must have got the orders mixed up."

Tilly empathised with his problem. "I appreciate how difficult it must be when you're as busy as this; will it take long to change?"

"Well, I can't say; perhaps you'd like something else instead?"

Tilly thought about it, but rejected the idea. "No thank you, I'd still like a medium steak — they are always really good here. I'd like it as soon as possible."

Being clear and direct meant that both parties felt good; the waiter felt valued for doing a difficult job, and Tilly was pleased that she had spoken up.

It is not always possible or appropriate to be assertive in all situations, but, having considered all the different options, we find that assertiveness usually reveals itself as being the most effective. Having accepted this, we now need to look at the skills which enable us to be more assertive.

3 Being Assertive

Introduction

Assertiveness comes complete with its own toolkit — an extremely useful set of verbal and non-verbal skills which enable us to communicate more effectively.

THE TOOLKIT

Body language
Setting the scene
Disclosing feelings
Being clear
Staying with it
Empathising
Working for a compromise

Body Language

We need to develop an awareness of our body language in order to communicate assertively. Research tells us that at least three-quarters of our communication occurs at this non-verbal level. A mismatch between our verbal and non-verbal messages reduces the effectiveness of what we are trying to say.

Because we cannot see our own body language, we need to receive feedback from others and role-play provides an excellent opportunity to do this.

Daisy needed to return some trousers as the zip had broken the first time she wore them. As she felt nervous about doing this, she took the opportunity to role-play the situation during one of the group sessions. She walked rather hesitantly into 'the shop' and finally attracted the attention of 'the assistant'. Her request to exchange the trousers was clear and specific, but her embarrassment meant that she was not looking at the assistant, but down at the floor. She stood off-balance, giving an impression of hesitancy and unsureness, and fiddled constantly with her earrings. The observers in Daisy's group gave her feedback about her inconsistent body language and the effect it had on them. With these points in mind, Daisy role-played the situation again. This time she walked confidently into 'the shop' with her head held high and went directly up to 'the assistant'. She made sure that she kept eye contact and reminded herself not to fidget. The difference was remarkable. Simply by ensuring that her non-verbal and verbal messages matched, she was much more assertive.

Feeling strong and balanced, with feet firmly planted, helps to give us a sense of equality and conveys confidence in what we are doing. Keeping direct comfortable eye contact is an open and honest form of communication. Our eyes cannot lie as easily as our mouths. Unnecessary gestures can be distracting and may reveal our anxiety, whereas confident gestures which emphasise what we are saying reinforce our verbal message.

We need to respect each other's body space and not invade it. Standing too close can be very intimidating, just as standing too far away can give an impression of detachment and lack of interest.

It is a common occurrence to find ourselves smiling, when in fact we feel angry inside, and we often say 'No' firmly and clearly whilst all the time our heads are nodding assent. Being aware of our body language is the first step in enabling us to make the small changes which are often all that are required to ensure we give an assertive message.

Assertive communication is about equality, so we need to ensure that we talk to people on an equal level physically, by adjusting our height to theirs. This is especially important when talking to wheelchair users, children or people of diminished growth.

Perhaps the most important aspect of body language is the way we use our voice. Our intonation can make all the difference; saying something with a sarcastic edge to our voice will reveal our underlying aggression, even if the words are assertive. The speed of our speech often reveals our anxiety; slowing it down helps us to sound calm and assertive. We need to ensure that our voices are loud enough — even an assertive response will have no effect if it cannot be heard. In the same way, it can be useful to check if we are speaking too loudly, as this often gives an aggressive message when none was intended.

Our body language is always affected by the way we feel. Even if we try hard to deny and repress our feelings, they will leak out somewhere, somehow. A verbal denial, such as "Of course it doesn't matter that you're late", does not ring true as we angrily stomp off down the hall to rescue the burnt dinner.

Setting the Scene

This is the art of feeling in control of a situation, allowing us the maximum opportunity for an assertive outcome. Feeling strong comes from feeling prepared, so clarify to yourself what you want to say and how you are going to say it. Wherever possible, *you* choose the place and the time to meet, and be sure you have a clear idea of what you want.

Mohammed was an out-patient attending weekly therapy sessions in a mental health centre. His doctor had suggested that he continue his course of anti-depressants, something which Mohammed felt unhappy about. He decided to make his feelings known to the doctor, and chose a time when he knew he could see him privately without interruption. Before he went, he wrote down all the points he wanted to make, and decided what he would like to gain from the meeting.

Disclosing Feelings

Making our feelings known to others is not the easiest of skills, but it is one of the most effective. By using 'I' statements we take responsibility for the feeling we are expressing. These feelings can be negative or positive. What is important is that we express them honestly, without blaming other people for them.

When Mohammed met the doctor he began by disclosing his feelings: "I feel really anxious about seeing you." This disclosure gave him a sense of relief and helped the doctor empathise with the way he felt.

Being Clear

Speaking in a way which communicates to others exactly what we mean is a fundamental assertive skill. When we are unsure we tend to pad out our statements unnecessarily. Concise, specific speech is assertive, and when our meaning is clear we are communicating most effectively with others.

After disclosing his feelings, Mohammed continued, "I've given this a lot of thought and I've decided I don't wish to continue with my drugs." Mohammed had made himself very clear and the doctor was left in no doubt as to what he wanted.

Staying with it and Empathising

We describe these two skills together as it is appropriate for them to be used in conjunction. *Staying with it* is the art of persisting with your request or statement and resisting being side-tracked, something which often happens when we are feeling vulnerable or pressurised. *Empathising* involves a verbal acknowledgement of the other person's position or feelings, thus demonstrating a genuine respect for the rights of others and an understanding of their point of view.

Used together these skills enable us to avoid getting hooked by irrelevant or manipulative comments, and to work towards a resolution of the problem.

After listening to what Mohammed had to say, the doctor responded, "I think you still need them; you're not better yet, you know."

Mohammed replied, "I realise you don't think I'm cured and you'd like me to carry on, but I do feel much better and I'm sure I can manage without them."

The doctor continued, "But I feel sure the tablets will help you. You are really not helping yourself if you refuse, you know."

Mohammed replied, "I realise you are trying to help me. I just don't want to take the tablets any more. I'd really like to try without them."

By empathising with the doctor's remarks, he showed that he had both heard what was being said and acknowledged that the doctor had his interests at heart. By staying with his message he was coming across strongly and clearly.

Working for a Compromise

Our desire to win in a particular situation can mean that we sometimes avoid using this extremely useful skill. Appreciating the other person's position means that we can often resolve a problem by reaching a mutually agreed conclusion. Both parties are then left feeling satisfied.

> The doctor was still not happy with Mohammed's decision. "I can see that you're really against this idea, but I'm worried about you stopping the tablets straight away."
>
> Mohammed responded, "I appreciate your concern, but I'd like to stop taking them by the end of the month. Could you advise me as to how I can cut them down gradually?"
>
> The doctor thought for a moment and then replied, "Yes I could do that; I'm willing to give it a try, but I'd like to see you every week when you come up for therapy."

Working for a compromise is an effective means of reaching a solution and avoiding a stalemate, as the above example demonstrates. For Mohammed to feel confident enough to discuss this matter with his doctor he needed to believe in his right to be assertive, the subject of our next chapter.

4 Our Right to be Assertive

Introduction

Behaving assertively requires the belief that we all have certain basic human rights, as this is the basis of the whole philosophy of assertive behaviour. Aggressive behaviour involves the violation of other people's rights, whereas behaving passively means we allow our rights to be violated. Assertive behaviour entails standing up for our own rights while respecting those of others.

The Rights Charter

You will find a list of rights in every book on assertiveness; this is the list that we use, presented as a charter.

THE RIGHTS CHARTER

1 I have the right to be treated with respect as an equal human being.

2 I have the right to acknowledge my needs as being equal to those of others.

3 I have the right to express my opinions, thoughts and feelings.

4 I have the right to make mistakes.

5 I have the right to choose not to take responsibility for other people.

6 I have the right to be me without being dependent on the approval of others.

This list is by no means exhaustive and, as you will see in Appendix I, we have included an exercise on the compilation of rights which are personal to each individual or group, which you may find useful.

Many people find acceptance of the rights difficult. Their heads are full of messages, such as 'I can't contradict him, he's the doctor'; 'If I say I don't understand, they'll think I'm stupid'; 'It will upset my friend if I ask her not to smoke in my house'. Accepting the basic bill of rights helps us to choose the assertive option.

Often this will be the first time some of our clients will ever have considered that they have rights at all. For many people becoming aware of rights can prove to be an extremely powerful experience. Acceptance is rarely an overnight process — it can take time for the ideas to sink in. Considering which right is being exercised at the beginning of every role-play is an effective way of reminding people of its significance.

In order to illustrate the power of the rights message we have used clients' own examples of demonstrating their right to be assertive:

---

1 I have the right to be treated with respect as an equal human being

---

Although this right appears fundamental, unfortunately we live in a very unequal world which rates some people as better than others for all sorts of reasons. **Alberti and Emmons** write about this in their book, *Your Perfect Right*, and give a list of generally accepted assumptions:

▶ Men are better than women
▶ Whites are better than blacks

▶ Adults are better than children
▶ Bosses are better than employees

To this list we would add the following:

▶ Doctors are better than patients
▶ Fluent speakers are better than stammerers
▶ Able-bodied people are better than the disabled
▶ Heterosexuals are better than homosexuals
▶ Well people are better than the ill
▶ Therapists are better than their clients

The list is endless. These ideas are deeply embedded in our belief systems. It is one thing to be told we are equal, but quite another to feel it in the face of such strong messages.

> Arthur was told by his consultant that he needed yet another operation to straighten his deformed arm. "I want you in hospital next week to sort this out," he was told.
>
> He had arranged to go on an adventure holiday with a group of other disabled people from the Sports Club. Canoeing and abseiling with an arm in plaster would be impossible. Thinking through the 'equal rights' issue helped him to go back to the consultant, state his case and put off the operation until after the holiday.

"I would never have dared to do that before; I always considered myself to be inferior to people like doctors."

The respect he felt for himself encouraged him to 'feel equal' as a disabled person in an 'unequal' society.

---

2 I have the right to acknowledge my needs as being equal to those of others

This can be a difficult concept for many people to absorb. So often in our society the message comes through that putting others first is the 'right' way to behave. Women, especially, can be caught in this trap of compassion as they assume the major part of the caring role within their family.

Many women suffer anxiety and depression, which can often be traced back to a history of passivity and an inability to see their needs as equal to those of others. Acknowledging that our needs are important, and learning how to state them, can have a dramatic effect on the quality of our lives.

> Olivia felt tired and pressured; she had had a hard day at work and was faced with an evening spent clearing up the bedroom, which had just been decorated. When Anne telephoned at four o'clock to ask if she and Mike could come round later for a drink she found herself saying, "Yes, of course, it will be lovely to see you."
>
> Despair set in as soon as she replaced the receiver: "Why did I do that — I need this evening to myself."
>
> On reflection she realised that her 'unselfish' act would probably rebound on her, as she would be unable to hide her tiredness and resentment during the visit. She rang Anne back, explained the situation and arranged a meeting later in the week.

Responsible assertive behaviour acknowledges that our needs are as important as other people's; not greater, or lesser, just equal.

---

3 I have the right to express my opinions, thoughts and feelings

Perhaps we should add here — 'even if they are in conflict with those of other people'. It is one thing to talk about your opinions on vegan food at a meeting of the Vegan Society, but quite another to do it at a Butchers' Convention! We often think that our ideas are not as worthwhile or as important as the next person's. Allowing ourselves to express our thoughts, opinions and feelings, whatever they may be, is a means of confirming and valuing ourselves. It is perfectly reasonable for us to express whatever we feel without having to justify it. We may have a different opinion from someone else, we may feel angry or sad, we may want to share our thoughts or keep them to ourselves, but if we accept that we have the right to express them we can choose whether we wish to do so or not.

Cheryl had been married for 20 years to a man who always put forward his ideas vociferously and often ended by saying "And that is that!" She told the group how often she disagreed but never said so; after all, he was more intelligent, capable and knowledgeable than she was. She used to walk away from the discussion, saying to herself that she did not agree with him. Finally she had the courage to speak the unspeakable and explain how she felt differently about things. She had to say it three times before he heard her, but then he acknowledged her point and walked away. "I know I still have a long way to go, but I feel this is the start. It is the first time I have felt on the same level as him in 20 years."

4 I have the right to make mistakes

We all make mistakes — nobody is perfect — but it can prove very difficult to admit the fact. Children learn very early in life that 'getting it right' is what is important: you do not gain any Brownie points for failing.

The development of a strong feeling of self-worth, intrinsic to behaving assertively, helps us to admit our errors without feeling ashamed or diminished. We can learn so much from our mistakes. Giving people permission to admit them during a training session can prove to be an extremely positive experience.

Dorothy was a senior occupational therapist in a busy hospital department. She was responsible for ordering new equipment and had a reputation for efficiency which she was proud of. When she was asked by her manager for the new bath aids she realised with a shock that she had forgotten to post the order.

"My first instinct was to fob her off with an excuse and 'phone the order through, but I remembered that I had the right to make a mistake; I realised I wasn't being honest, either with her or myself."

Admitting to her mistake gave her a great sense of relief and encouraged a more open relationship with her manager.

5 I have the right to choose not to take responsibility for other people

As therapists this is one of the hardest lessons for us to learn; adopting an assertive outlook in our work means that we prefer to help our clients take on responsibility for themselves and their own problems rather than trying to solve everything our way. This taking responsibility for solving other people's problems is an aggressive way of acting, as it violates another person's right to be themselves.

Attached to this right is the risk of being called uncaring and selfish — labels which can hurt. In fact nothing could be further from the truth than such accusations. If we continue obsessively to take on other people's problems we end up with little energy for ourselves or anyone else. We need to set a limit on how far we feel we can go.

Irene had a brother living at the other end of the country. He was disabled following a stroke and needed constant care. Irene took on responsibility for all his problems, something that was well nigh impossible at a distance of 200 miles; so the inevitable happened and she left her own home and went to live with him. It was a complete disaster. The small amount of independence and autonomy he had vanished overnight as Irene 'unselfishly' took over his life. The experiment lasted for three months, before she returned home, exhausted and bewildered. Discussing the problem in the group helped her to come to a decision which suited both parties. She offered support, encouragement and financial assistance from a distance, thus allowing her brother to find solutions to his own problems and so retain the independence which was so important to his self-respect.

---

6 I have the right to be me without being dependent on the approval of others

---

When discussing this right in the various groups we have run, it often emerges as the most difficult one for people to accept. Our early conditioning results in women, especially, becoming caught up in the idea that pleasing other people is more important than pleasing themselves. This is one of the reasons why we find it so hard to say 'No' to people, to walk out of the shoe shop when the assistant has brought us 12 pairs of shoes without complaint. There is a deep underlying fear of not being liked and admired by everyone we meet, which, if you consider the implications, is quite irrational.

Natalie Shainess in *Sweet Suffering*, devotes a chapter to the way women put themselves into positions of danger through their overwhelming need for approval. She cites the example of waiting for the lift in a multi-storey car park. A man comes to wait beside you. "I don't like the look of him. I feel scared, but I can't walk away now — he'll think I'm being funny." So you get in the lift — you might be safe, but equally you might not.

A useful technique to help people begin to break this dependency on approval is to get them to ask themselves two questions. Do I like everyone I meet? Answer: of course not. It is not possible to do so. Then why do I operate on the expectation that everyone I meet will like me?

Once people have accepted the 'rights charter' there can be a danger of them becoming 'rights conscious', seeing every violation of their rights as outrageous and unforgivable. This is an aggressive rather than an assertive response and it helps to point this out whenever the rights session is being presented. Assertive behaviour involves respecting the rights of others as well as ourselves, even when we disagree with them. An example we often use is that of someone making racist remarks within our hearing. The person has the right to hold and express these opinions, just as we have the right to tell them how we feel when those opinions are expressed and to assert that our views are different.

Assertive Thought

Assertive thought is the practice of thinking positively about ourselves and our lives. It is an essential first step towards behaving assertively. Giving ourselves negative internal messages will result in negative behaviour. Telling yourself "I will never be able to pass" is the surest way of failing a driving test. We so often set ourselves up for failure. Acknowledging and believing in our rights as individuals enables us to think more assertively.

> Josh was standing in a queue at the supermarket when someone pushed in front of him.
>
> "I took a breath, and remembered my rights, telling myself it was OK for me to let this person know how I felt."
>
> He was able to say that he felt annoyed at them jumping the queue, and asked them to take their place.

Thinking of what we want to say beforehand in a situation is a vital step towards behaving assertively, but our ability to do this is often clouded by negative thought patterns: "I can't say anything", "It's not worth it", "People will think I'm awful." Thinking in this way makes it even harder to think of what we want to say, and to say it clearly.

When we find ourselves thinking negatively, it is important that we challenge ourselves. Turning the thought from a negative to a positive has a very real effect on our self-esteem. Faced with a situation where we feel vulnerable, we are far more likely to be able to deal with it if we can give ourselves a boost by thinking positively. As human beings we are well qualified in the art of putting ourselves down and denying our strengths. "I'll never be able to do it" can be challenged by a positive thought, such as "I'll have a go at this and see how I get on." This can mean the difference between feeling fine or feeling downcast, coping or feeling hopeless, being assertive or being passive.

There are many emotive words in our vocabulary which prevent us from thinking assertively and thus being assertive. **Albert Ellis**, in *Reason and Emotion in Psychotherapy*, presents the notion of Rational Emotive Therapy — encouraging an individual to challenge negative thoughts to improve their sense of well-being and effectiveness in life. We use words such as '*should*', '*ought*' and '*must*' which are laced with feelings of guilt and duty. Replacing such words with '*could*', '*want to*' and '*can*' is empowering and freeing.

> Rosemary was an overweight woman who was receiving counselling. When she repeatedly told herself "I must lose weight", "I should not eat so much", she trapped herself into a pattern of guilty negative thinking. Taking control of her problem by saying to herself "I would like to lose weight", and qualifying it by adding "but I find it difficult", "I want to eat less and I can try to do that", gave her a sense of acceptance and permission which had previously been absent. By consistently challenging her thinking she was eventually able to confront her over-eating and gradually began to lose weight.

Feeling good by accepting ourselves for who we are, 'warts and all', is central to assertive behaviour. Our right to express our feelings is something that we look at in more detail in the next chapter.

5 Owning our Feelings

Introduction

We all have the right to express our feelings, whatever they may be. 'Owning' our feelings means taking responsibility both for acknowledging what we feel and for the way we act on it. It is important that we learn to accept our feelings, however strong or frightening they are, and that we are prepared to express them openly and honestly.

What are Feelings?

Feelings are both physical and emotional sensations within our bodies. Learning to recognise the physical changes which occur helps us to identify more clearly what our emotional state is.

Physical change	Emotional state
sweating heart pounding fast and erratic breathing churning stomach	anxiety
warmth surging energy strong heart beat relaxed muscles	happiness

Physical change	Emotional state
heaviness lethargy fatigue tearfulness	 depression

We live in a society that gives little permission for the safe expression of feelings. We often grow up with messages such as 'anger is bad' and 'compassion is good'. By labelling feelings in this way we are encouraged to acknowledge only those we are told are good and to deny or repress those we have been told are bad. This means that we are often tempted to concentrate negatively on feelings such as anger, pain and grief. We frequently tell ourselves how unhappy we are, and rarely celebrate our feelings of joy and love. Assertiveness encourages us to see and share the positive aspects of our lives.

Each culture handles feelings differently: contrast the mourners at an Islamic funeral with those at a British one and we can see and hear a vast difference. Mourners at an Islamic funeral openly moan and wail for their loved ones, whereas in Britain it is far more usual to hear an occasional sob and see a discreet dabbing of the eye.

Denial and Repression

People have often been taught that showing emotions is a weakness, rather than a strength, whereas we believe the opposite to be true. Repression of feelings can be destructive, both for our minds and for our bodies. Unexpressed anger, frustration or guilt can lead to anxiety and depression and there is also evidence emerging of physical diseases such as cancer and asthma being linked to the continuous repression of feelings. Repressed feelings are often restimulated in us when we least expect it. A song, a smell or a photograph can be enough to trigger off emotions that have lain buried inside us for many years.

Many of us bottle up our feelings instead of expressing them at the appropriate time, thinking that they are so well hidden inside us that they will never emerge. But beware — feelings always find an escape route!

Josie had been married for 15 years. She had spent her life looking after the needs of her husband and family, receiving very little acknowledgement for it. To avoid conflict she bottled up all her anger, never really saying how she felt, which contributed to her bouts of depression. After several months of therapy it became clear that her underlying unexpressed anger was at the root of her condition. Through attending an assertiveness group, Josie learned how to express her anger openly and honestly. She began to accept anger as a permissible emotion, and grew in her confidence to deal with anger assertively.

Handling feelings assertively involves three stages: acknowledgement, disclosure and physical release.

Acknowledgement

It is often difficult for us to identify what we are feeling. Physical sensations are the signposts which indicate our emotions: the more we learn to take note of them, the easier identification becomes. It is easier to admit to joy than to jealousy, but unless we acknowledge for ourselves that the feeling exists, we may not be able to express it honestly and constructively.

> Jackie often felt intensely jealous whenever Peter talked about his previous relationships. She never said anything, but would immediately change the subject and look disapproving. As Peter grew more uncertain about her reaction, Jackie's jealousy grew deeper. When he eventually asked her why she was so upset he was met with a vehement denial that anything was wrong. Jackie was failing to acknowledge her own jealousy.

Disclosure

We often assume that people know how we feel, especially in a close relationship; there can be an expectation that one partner knows how the other one is feeling. When this is not the case it can lead us to experience hurt and rejection.

> Jeremy had had a hard day at work and he felt tired and frustrated. When he came home his partner announced excitedly that he had arranged an evening out for them with friends. Jeremy went off to get ready, thinking, "What a time to choose; doesn't he realise how tired and tense I am? He hasn't got any consideration for my feelings!"

We cannot rely on people reading our minds. It is our responsibility to tell them how we feel. When we do this, it is important that we take full responsibility for our feelings, without blaming them on other people. For example, "You make me feel angry when you talk about me behind my back" is aggressive rather than assertive. True self-disclosure involves the use of 'I' statements: "I feel cross when you don't tidy up your room." This has a completely different effect, showing that the speaker is taking responsibility for themselves and how they feel.

When we share our feelings verbally we are, to some degree, releasing them. Disclosing our anxiety at the beginning of a speech helps us to feel less anxious about making it. It is important, however, that our self-disclosure is honest, and appropriate to the feeling we have. If we say we are a little upset, when in fact we are absolutely furious, our inappropriate self-disclosure will leave us with most of the feeling still bottled up inside.

One of our greatest fears about telling people how we feel is that we are making ourselves vulnerable and opening ourselves up to possible manipulation and rejection. Assertiveness involves taking risks, and this is one of them. But we stand to lose far more by not sharing with those close to us than we would gain from keeping silent and swallowing our feelings.

Physical Release

Physically expressing our feelings is fraught with the same cultural and social taboos that prevent us from acknowledging them. There are often strong messages to both sexes about physically releasing feelings:

▶ Men don't cry

▶ Women don't get angry

▶ Men don't touch other men

▶ Women don't shout

We need to challenge these messages for ourselves, so that we can be comfortable about releasing powerful emotions such as anger, frustration, jealousy and grief.

We can learn to physically let go of our feelings in a constructive and safe way. Some of the methods suggested by group members are:

▶ Strenuous physical exercise

▶ Gardening

▶ An energetic cleaning session

▶ Screaming into a cushion

▶ Beating a pillow with your fists

▶ Crying and sobbing

▶ Using relaxation

Obviously it is not always possible to use some of these techniques at the time we feel most strongly, as we need a degree of privacy to feel safe enough to release our feelings. However we can always use relaxation, wherever we are and whatever the situation. There are many exercises on relaxation; we have suggested a few in Appendix I which you may like to use with your groups.

Cognitive Release

There are several other ways of releasing our emotions constructively. Thinking things through after the event, reflecting on what has happened and how we felt can help us to let go of the emotions. We often hang on to the negative thoughts and events, carrying them around with us like bricks in a rucksack. Letting go takes practice; it means being able to leave something behind you and to free yourself of the emotion. Learning to meditate can help us to achieve this. Rationalising the event and putting it into perspective can also be useful. Try seeing the situation for what it really is, rather than allowing exaggeration and negative emphasis to further the feelings, as we have discussed in the section on assertive thought (*see p15*). Writing is often an effective way of pouring our thoughts and feelings out onto paper. For some of us diaries can prove to be invaluable. Drawing is another way of projecting our emotions. Talking through a problem and allowing our feelings to come to the surface can be really productive. It can help us to clarify how we feel, but it is not a substitute for honestly disclosing our feelings to the person who has upset us.

Remembering our right to share our feelings and not being scared to take responsibility for them is an essential aspect of assertive communication. In the next chapter we look at ways in which we can offer refusals and make requests in a similarly assertive and honest manner.

6 Refusing and Requesting

Introduction

Assertive communication is not only a matter of asking clearly for what we want — it also involves stating firmly what we do not want. Most of this chapter is devoted to refusing requests, rather than making them. People nearly always bring at least one example of saying 'No' to role-play in any group. 'No' is such a simple word, yet it can prove so difficult to say. Considering that it is one of the first words we learn to speak as children, it is clearly not a case of 'practice making perfect'!

> Carol told the group that she felt something of a fraud in coming to the workshop as she was already able to be assertive in many situations. However her one stumbling-block was saying 'No' to people. Each time she tried it, she felt great pangs of anxiety and guilt.

> This overwhelming sense of guilt about saying 'No' can be seen again and again when working with clients. To understand the strength of these feelings, we need to look at the beliefs which underlie them.

The Belief Beneath the Feeling

Belief number one: "Saying no means they'll think I'm selfish."

Most of us have been brought up with the idea that caring for others is more important than caring for ourselves. From childhood we are taught that it is wrong to put our own needs first. Behaving in this way is often classed as selfish, even impolite, and frequently carries with it an underlying fear of rejection: "If I behave selfishly nobody will like me." Our need for approval is so strong that we can be spurred into constantly offering our time, our energy and ourselves in an attempt to gain praise and love from others in order to boost our self-esteem.

Belief number two: **"I can't say 'no' because I must always help other people."**

When we place the emphasis on 'I should', 'I must', 'I ought' we can be sure that this signals strongly held beliefs which have been drummed into us from childhood. Carol described it very well: "I feel as though I have my mother sitting on one shoulder, my grandmother on the other and God on my head, all of them whispering the same messages in my ears: I should be helpful and kind to everyone; I must always be generous and unselfish; I ought to look after others' needs first."

Acting on these messages results in us being labelled in very positive ways:

Dependable friends

Helpful neighbours

Devoted partners

Untiring workers

Wonderful mothers

It feels good to receive praise like this, but subjugating our needs to those of others all the time means that we walk into the trap of never being able to say 'No', no matter how inconvenient, awkward or distasteful the request may be. As we pointed out earlier, women, especially, can experience enormous difficulty in freeing themselves from this trap of compassion.

Acting assertively means challenging these beliefs and allowing ourselves to let go of our need for constant approval.

Belief number three: **"I couldn't possibly say 'no' — it would hurt their feelings."**

We often offer this as a reason for not saying 'No'. Our early learning can lead us into being protective of others' feelings, at the expense of our own. We find ourselves spending time with people we do not want to be with, and in situations not of our choosing. Although we may say 'Yes', our true feelings will tend to leak out through our body language.

Having accepted an invitation to a noisy disco on a night Mark really wanted to spend alone, he was not surprised to find a headache developing as he sat alone at a table, feeling guilty for not joining in the fun, in order not to hurt his friend's feelings. He realised that he was poor company, and recognised that an honest refusal would have been better all round.

There are many other beliefs which fuel our resistance to refusing requests. We have described the three we believe to be the most common, but there are others linked to them which may be presented to you.

Challenging the Belief

Before we can begin to say 'No', we need to challenge these beliefs.

The belief: **"Saying no means they'll think I'm selfish."**
The challenge: **"By looking after myself I'm more able to look after others."**

Someone at a party once asked us, "Tell me, just what is the difference between assertiveness and selfishness?" When we act selfishly we only look after our own needs. Being assertive involves taking equal care of our own and others' needs. By making ourselves constantly available, we run the risk of becoming exhausted and resentful — hardly a good basis from which to give to others. By looking after ourselves we can develop the strength which enables us to reach out willingly to those we choose to help.

> Moira's telephone rang most evenings just as she was involved in preparing her evening meal. Nine times out of ten it would be Sally, her neighbour, ringing to talk about her traumatic divorce. One Thursday, after answering and hearing the familiar voice, Moira put her dinner back into the oven for the second time that week. She began to feel resentment building up inside her; unable to take in any of her friend's long list of troubles, she concentrated on getting her off the telephone as quickly as possible. Two days later, when it rang again, Moira decided to be assertive.
>
> *Sally*: Oh Moira, you'll never guess what happened at the solicitors today . . .
>
> *Moira*: I feel guilty saying this Sally, but it's really not convenient for me to talk now, I'm about to have dinner . . .
>
> *Sally*: Oh, I'm really sorry, I've obviously rung at a bad time. I'll ring you again in half an hour . . .
>
> *Moira*: No, I'd rather you didn't 'phone again tonight Sally, but I would like to know what the solicitor said. How about meeting tomorrow for lunch, when we've both got more time?

Moira was valuing herself and her friend by recognising that their needs had equal importance.

The belief: "I can't say 'no' because I must always help other people."
The challenge: "I can choose to help others if I wish."

We need to believe in the basic assertive assumption that our needs are equal, and that we have a right to make choices. Sometimes, however, there is little choice, as the other person's need is obviously greater than our own:

▶ You have a seat booked at the theatre and your babysitter can't make it;
▶ You had planned a day off work and the whole department is decimated by 'flu;
▶ You are late for work and your partner's car won't start.

The difficulty arises when both people's needs are pressing:

▶ You want to go on holiday in September; your children prefer August;
▶ You want to smoke during staff meetings; your colleagues disapprove;
▶ Your partner is offered work in the South and you want to stay in the North.

Saying 'No' to someone you've always said 'Yes' to is generally much more difficult.

> Fleur was just finishing a very heavy morning's work, and was looking forward to lunch with her friend, when the telephone rang. It was her mother, who lived six miles away in the next town.
>
> "Fleur, dear, I'm not feeling very well again — I had to call out the doctor this morning. It's this 'flu that's going round."
>
> "I'm sorry to hear that, mum; did she give you anything for it?"
>
> "Yes she did, a prescription for some pills, but I'm far too ill to go and get them; Mrs Garvey next door said she would go, but I told her not to bother because you'd come and get them in your lunch hour."
>
> In the past, Fleur had always dropped everything and run to help her mother, feeling very resentful afterwards. This time she decided to offer a compromise: "That's not possible today, mum, I've arranged something for this lunchtime. Could you take up Mrs Garvey's offer and I'll call tonight after work to see how you are?"
>
> "Really, Fleur, I thought you'd be glad to help me; I'm not a bit well."
>
> "I do want to help, mum, that's why I'm suggesting this evening, when I'll have more time to spend with you."

Fleur might well have decided to comply with her mother's request, deciding that her needs were greater, but, having made the alternative decision, she would be far more likely to offer her help without feeling resentful or put upon. Some days the assertive option is easier to take than others, and this is an important point, worth stressing to your clients.

The belief: **"I couldn't possibly say 'no' — it would hurt their feelings."**
The challenge: **"I'm not responsible for other people's feelings."**

If people feel hurt by our refusals, this is not our responsibility, just as it is not theirs if we feel hurt when they refuse us. Those of us lucky enough to know someone who can say 'No' to us clearly and directly will recognise the value of this. As one of our clients puts it: "I have a friend who will always say 'No' when she wants to; knowing this makes her 'Yes' far more valuable. Whether she says 'No' or 'Yes', I know she means it wholeheartedly."

It is an unhealthy relationship which depends on one party constantly discounting their own desires to please the other. We find it really useful to point out to our clients a quote from **Anne Dickson**: "When we say no, we are refusing the request, not rejecting the person."

Setting Limits

Before we say 'No' to anyone we need to have a clear idea of our own personal limits. How far we are prepared to go in any situation will depend on a variety of factors. The boundaries will be different for each of us, and depend on our own personal circumstances. This needs to be stressed, as clients sometimes feel pressurised into conforming to others' limits rather than acknowledging and setting their own.

▶ I prefer to know in advance when friends are calling, whereas you are happy to have them drop round anytime.

▶ You welcome working overtime, whereas I choose not to.

▶ We don't give our children regular pocket money, whereas you give yours some every week.

Making our limits known means that we are more likely to say 'No' and keep to it.

Ways of Saying 'No'

When we do decide to turn down someone's request, we are rarely specific about it. A clear 'No' is seldom heard; instead we use a complex set of excuses, lies and justification. These can leave both parties feeling bad and often rebound on us at some future date. The examples on the next page show the trouble we can get into.

The first thing to do when saying 'No' is to clarify what we really want by listening to our feelings. When our spirits rise after hearing the request, the chances are we want to say 'Yes'; if our stomach plummets to the floor, we can be certain a 'No' is what we are looking for.

Response	Result
"Sorry, I can't have the kids. It's not that I don't want them, don't get me wrong, it's just that I'd promised to run Jane to her gym class, and then I've got the garden to weed and the dog to take out and a hundred and one other things to do . . ."	"I get the message . . . sorry I even asked."
"What a shame, I'd love to come to the party, but Bob's aunt is staying so she'll be with us this weekend."	"How fortunate — you can bring her along; she'll be company for my mother."

Often people ask us to make decisions on very little information; we can always ask for further explanation: "How long do I have to work on a Saturday?"; "When do you want the printing to be ready?"; "What exactly are the duties involved in being a volunteer?" Another thing we can ask for is time. Decisions made under pressure often turn out to be the wrong ones. Ask for time to consider a request, and then use that time to reflect, gather more information or ask for advice: "I'd like time to consider your idea of a job share; I'll give it some thought and get back to you on Monday morning by 10 o'clock"; "Your special offer sounds very attractive. However I don't want to make a decision here and now. If you call on Friday I can give you a definite answer."

When we make a refusal we need to ensure that we use the word 'No' in our response, and that our body language is complementary, rather than contradictory. Saying 'No' involves using a clear definitive 'No', an honest expression of feelings and, if necessary, a simple explanation: "No, I can't help this time, I'm sorry. I hope you have a successful show"; "I feel guilty saying 'no'; however I've decided to spend this weekend with my children."

Learning to say 'No' brings immense benefits. In our experience the guilt is always present. We cannot promise that it will ever go away completely, but it does diminish in time.

Making Requests

Asking for our needs to be met is more difficult when our self-esteem is low. If we do not value ourselves we are unlikely to ask for what we want. As our self-esteem grows, our ability to make requests increases. Assertive communication involves making clear, direct requests, which leave people in no doubt as to what we want. This directness is often discouraged, being perceived to be rude and pushy; as a result, dropping hints and insinuating has become much more acceptable.

Hint	Assertive Request
"It's not far to Skegness and they say it's lovely at this time of year."	"Can we go to Skegness this weekend?"
"Isn't it smoky in here; I can't stop coughing."	"I'd like to go to another bar, this one's too smoky."
"I'm sick to death of all this *!*! washing up."	"Please would you help me with this washing up?"

There is no guarantee that our requests will always be met. Every time we ask for what we want, we risk a refusal. However our chances are greatly improved if we ask clearly and directly. Failing to do this means that we deny our own importance, and negate our rights as individuals.

Lillian had always found it difficult to ask others for help, believing that others had more right to state their needs than she did. Attending an assertiveness group helped her to realise that she had a right to ask for what she wanted. With this new-found understanding she decided to approach her partner, to ask him for more help with the children at the weekends, leaving her with some time for herself. Lillian was pleasantly surprised by his positive response, and felt encouraged to state her needs more often in the future.

Making requests assertively both increases and reflects our level of self-respect, the importance of which we consider in the next chapter.

7 Self-respect

Self love my liege is not so vile a sin as self neglect.
WILLIAM SHAKESPEARE

Introduction

Respecting and valuing ourselves and having positive self-esteem is one of the corner-stones on which assertive behaviour is built. As professionals we need to be aware of our own degree of self-esteem and how it affects us and those around us. Traumatic or disabling events in our lives can lead to a diminished level of self-respect. Our clients are often disabled further by being treated with prejudice and inequality, with the effect of further destroying their sense of self.

Each one of us is unique. Our healthiest option would be to accept ourselves as we are. Instead we spend most of our time comparing ourselves with others, trying to measure up to their expectations. When we are able to accept and value ourselves we can find greater peace and fulfilment in our lives. Having strong self-esteem is not believing that we are perfect, but rather accepting ourselves for who we are. Asking people to identify their positive and negative qualities usually results in a long list of negatives, with one or two positive points. Our embarrassment, inhibition and low self-confidence can make it very difficult for us to identify our strengths. Sometimes we hear ourselves making a positive statement, only to spoil it by ending it with a negative remark: "Yes, I am a good tennis player, but I should be, I've been playing for years."

Our level of self-esteem is affected by our experiences in our daily lives; the more we take risks, the more our self-respect increases.

Laura's self-confidence was consistently being knocked by the staff she worked with. She allowed herself to be exploited in the office, doing the jobs no one else wanted, and began to feel more and more worthless as time went on. After she had received individual assertiveness therapy her self-esteem developed to a level where she felt more confident in the office, and able to stand up for herself. She began to tackle things she had never thought she was capable of before. She learned to use the word processor and began to confront her colleagues' sarcastic remarks. With each step forward her self-confidence grew, and with it a greater sense of respect for herself.

Building Self-esteem

There are an infinite number of ways in which we can raise low self-esteem, and clients are often surprised at how similar their methods are. Some of the ideas quoted most often are:

▶ talking positively to myself;
▶ acknowledging my strengths;
▶ changing behaviour I am not happy with;
▶ celebrating behaviour I like;
▶ treating myself;
▶ looking after my health;
▶ taking space for myself;
▶ taking time to look at the world around me;
▶ seeking help and support when I need it;
▶ getting to know myself.

We have looked in more detail at different methods of building self-esteem in the exercises linked to this chapter.

Compliments

Giving and receiving compliments can be a very positive way of building our self-esteem. One of the first changes we noticed in ourselves as a result of our assertiveness training was an increase in the number of compliments we gave to those around us, and the increased ease with which we accepted them.

When giving a compliment, we are taking a risk: will the person accept it as a present caringly given, or treat it with suspicion and throw it back in our face? Unfortunately most of us find it hard to let the compliments in. The messages we have received over the years tell us that it is immodest and impolite to acknowledge a compliment, so we often brush it off in a variety of ways:

▶ By implying that we do not deserve it.
    Compliment: "Your suit is very smart."
    Response: "Oh this old thing, I've had it ages."

▶ By using humour to put the person down.
    Compliment: "You look nice today."
    Response: "Well, don't sound so surprised!"

▶ By focussing on the other person.

>*Compliment*: "I really liked your chocolate cake."
>
>*Response*: "Oh, but it's not as good as yours!"

These responses effectively reject both the person and their compliment. We can all find compliments difficult to accept, but some of our clients have particular difficulty, perhaps because they have had so little practice. We often feel suspicious of compliments, sometimes with good reason. There can be a feeling that we are being manipulated or buttered up and flattery often does precede a request of some kind: "You women are so efficient, I'm sure you won't mind organising the hospital dance for Friday."

A genuine compliment is easy to spot: it is said with sincerity and feeling. Our response needs to be just as genuine: "I really like your paintings." "Thank you, I'm pleased you like them." While accepting the compliment verbally, we need also to allow ourselves to internalise it, a very positive way of nurturing our self-esteem.

Loving and looking after ourselves is not an entirely selfish act; the quality of what we give to others is ultimately enhanced by our own self-respect. Having a strong sense of self-esteem is vital when dealing with criticism, the subject of our next chapter.

8 Criticism and Conflict

Receiving Criticism

Learning to handle criticism was one of the most positive aspects of our assertiveness training. One of the hardest concepts for us to grasp was that of criticism being a gift: how could something which causes us so much pain be thought of as a present? Yet feedback about the effect of our behaviour on others is truly a valuable gift. It affords us the chance to develop an awareness of ourselves, which otherwise we might never achieve. Choosing to change our behaviour as a result of this feedback can have a really positive effect on all our relationships, including the one we have with ourselves.

Before we can begin to see the positive side of criticism, we need to look at the reasons why we can normally only see it in a negative light.

Why Does It Hurt?

A helpful exercise is to ask people to recall the criticisms they received as children from their parents, teachers or other adults. Some of these criticisms would be levelled at:

▶ our **looks**:
   "You're so fat"
   "You've got legs like sticks"
   "Four eyes";

▶ our **intelligence**:
   "You're such a dunce"
   "What an idiot"
   "You're hopeless at spelling";

▶ and most certainly at our **behaviour**:
   "You're selfish"
   "You're soft"

"You're mean"

"You're wicked"

"You're silly"

"You're a wimp".

Notice how these criticisms are personalised and given to us as labels. We are not told, "That was a stupid thing to do", but rather "You are stupid." Is it any wonder that people ask, "Why do I take criticism so personally?" We can carry these labels with us into our adult lives, often retaining a particular one which still hurts us and upsets us many years later. These 'crumple buttons' can be triggered unwittingly by others' criticisms.

> Eva and Tony had lived together for over a year when they decided to rearrange the furniture in their living-room. As Tony moved a chair, he banged a small table, causing it to rock violently. "Don't be so damn clumsy, Tony, you nearly knocked that table over." This normally gentle, quiet man raged angrily at her, saying he wasn't clumsy, the table was in his way, and if she could do any better she was welcome to try. Discussing the incident later, Tony recalled his early teens when his mother had labelled him clumsy at every opportunity. The pain of that was still with him 23 years later.

As children we are so vulnerable. We rely on the adults around us for everything, both on a practical and an emotional level. Along with their criticisms of us we absorb the message that these 'defects' make us somehow unloveable. This sets up a fear that these all-powerful people, sitting in judgement on us, will withdraw their love and protection unless we can somehow learn to please them. They would often compare us with more 'satisfactory' children, sometimes our own brothers and sisters: "John would never have got all his sums wrong"; "Why can't you be more like Janet — she's so polite"; "It's a shame you are not pretty like your sister."

We spend a great deal of energy as adults in trying to measure up to others whom we perceive as being more perfect by constantly comparing ourselves with them. Building our self-esteem helps us to overcome the deep-rooted sense of rejection which threatens to overwhelm us each time we receive a criticism.

How to Handle it

Handling criticism assertively is something that we can all learn to do. Of course it is difficult not to react in the old conditioned ways we have been used to. Asking a group of clients how they usually respond to criticism will often elicit one of the behaviours shown on the table overleaf.

Reacting assertively, on the other hand, involves considering the criticism objectively, before giving a clear and honest response. The stages to go through are fairly simple but can be difficult to remember in that heart-stopping, stomach-churning moment when the criticism hits us. This is why it is important to allow clients time to learn to cope

---

Direct aggression

I always react defensively: "What do you mean I'm no good at it? I'd like to see you do any better."

Indirect aggression

I don't say anything, I just walk away and sulk.

Passivity

I believe they're right: "I'm terribly sorry, I know I'm hopeless. It's all my fault."

---

better with their own 'crumple buttons', by practising receiving criticism assertively within the safety of the group. There are four steps to follow:

Step One: Listen to the Criticism

It is essential to really listen to what is being said and to give ourselves time to consider the criticism. This helps us to avoid jumping immediately to our own defence, or swallowing the criticism whole, regardless of its truth or inaccuracy. Sometimes we are unsure of what people mean. If so, we need to ask them for clarification: "Can you give me a specific example?"; "I'm not sure what you mean; could you explain?"

Step Two: Decide on the Truth

Not all criticisms are true, so we need to check their validity before deciding how to react. The criticism may be *completely true, partly true, wholly untrue* or given in the form of a *put-down*; each will require a different response. When working with your clients, be aware that this requires a great deal of heart-searching. There can be a tendency to accept a criticism as true simply because we have heard it several times before, or because it is one of our labels from the past. Conversely we can deny it vehemently because admitting it would cause us too much pain. We see both these responses occurring in role-plays, and find that a helpful way of facilitating our clients is to encourage them to consider the validity of the criticism and thus to change their response. Quite often this results in a positive change in body language, as their honesty shows through.

Step Three: Respond Assertively

If the criticism is completely true we need to agree with it, without waffling or justifying. We may also wish to add a statement about how we feel and our plans for change: "You're right, I am untidy and I feel uncomfortable about it, so I'm trying hard to change." We can also enquire about the way our behaviour affects the other person: "You're right, I am untidy; it's not something that bothers me that much but how does it affect you?"

If the criticism is partly true we need to agree with the part we consider to be valid and then add a qualification: "I agree I can be selfish at times, but I'm not a totally selfish person." We can add a self-disclosure and an enquiry, as in the previous example: "Yes, I was late for this morning's meeting and I'm sorry, but I am not always late. Did it really mess things up for you?"

If the criticism is wholly untrue we need to disagree with it. Our statement needs to be a clear rejection of the criticism, followed by a positive personal affirmation: "No, I don't agree, I'm not lazy; I'm a very energetic person." Again we can add a self-disclosure and an enquiry: "No, I don't agree; I'm a very energetic person. I feel hurt by what you've said. What makes you think I'm lazy?"

This time our enquiry aims to discover how people have received this impression of us. The enquiry can either expose the criticism as an aggressive put-down or show that it is based on false information.

If the criticism is a put-down it needs to be handled differently. Put-downs are subtly malicious personal attacks. This indirect form of aggression often uses sarcasm or humour to disguise the real message: "You're a good driver for a woman"; "You're very young to be a manager"; "If you had brains you'd be dangerous"; "That's pretty good for you"; "You're very pretty, despite your size".

The use of humour can confuse us and consequently we do not always feel the pain immediately, often waking in the middle of the night, thinking, "So that's what she meant." When handling put-downs it is particularly important that we:

1 disclose our feelings:
"I feel really hurt by that remark",
"I feel offended by what you've said",
"I feel devastated by your comment";

2 ask them what they mean:
"I don't understand your comment. What do you mean?";
"I'm confused by what you've said. Could you explain?";

3 if appropriate, make a positive personal statement:
"I am a good driver. The fact that I'm a woman is irrelevant",
"Yes, I am young to be a manager. I believe I've done well in my career".

By challenging the put-down we expose the true intent. Either the person is making a deliberately malicious attack, or they are failing to realise the insensitivity of their remark.

Step Four: Letting Go

We tend to hang on to criticisms, adding them to the pile we have collected over the years. Assertiveness enables us to let them go. Letting go takes practice and becomes easier as our self-esteem develops.

Having recognised how painful criticism can be to hear, it becomes easier for us to empathise with those on the receiving end.

Giving Criticism

Giving criticism constructively is a skill relevant to us all. There are clearly defined steps to follow which, in our experience, can make the giving of criticism easier for both parties. Asking clients how they usually handle this will evoke the following responses.

The passive response is typified either by wrapping up the criticism so completely that it becomes obscured in the torrent of words: "Alice dear, I'm sorry to bother you, but I'd like a word about Jane. Now don't get me wrong, it's not that I don't like her to have sweets, I often give them to her myself, but not before dinner, at least not often; I wouldn't like to upset you, you're so good with her . . ."; or by simply saying nothing at all and putting up with whatever it is that angers or annoys us.

The directly aggressive response is usually a fierce personal attack, which blames the other person and passes judgement on them and their behaviour: "You ruined the whole party by your stupid behaviour. I would never carry on like that in front of people – you're really disgusting."

The indirectly aggressive response often uses emotional blackmail: "If you behave like this, you'll make me ill."

Any improvement on these methods must be worth considering! First we need to be clear about just what it is we are asking of the other person. We have said elsewhere that we cannot change others, only ourselves. However, where some aspect of their behaviour irritates, angers or inconveniences us, then we have the right to ask, in a constructive way, for a change. These are the steps to follow:

Step One

Check what you are saying to yourself. It is easy to work ourselves up into self-righteous anger, but all this does is provoke our own aggression. Instead we need to think of our rights, and acknowledge that the other person's are the same.

> Nigel was a nursing officer who needed to criticise one of his staff for being constantly late on duty. He found himself thinking: "What does Alison think she's playing at, she's not going to get away with this any longer," and then realised he was denying her the right to be treated with respect. Changing his thoughts to: "Alison's clearly got a problem at the moment which we need to get sorted out", helped him to approach the situation more positively.

Step Two

Choose the time and the place to talk things through. People are entitled to hear a criticism in private, not in front of a group of people in a busy corridor; we can find ourselves doing this, especially if we are anxious about the confrontation, and wanting to get it over as soon as possible.

Nigel arranged a mutually convenient time to meet with Alison in his office.

Step Three

Be specific in the criticism you give and avoid personalising it. Beware of making vague or generalised statements, which can act like a blanket thrown over us, leaving us feeling overwhelmed. Instead, make clear, non-judgemental statements.

> "Alison, you are arriving late for every shift, which means I have to keep rearranging the rota."

Step Four

Express your feelings about the behaviour that is troubling you, making sure you use the appropriate word to describe the strength of what you feel. Sometimes this self disclosure may come before the explanation, or after. No matter where it comes, it always has the same effect – it releases tension and anxiety and enables the other person to know how we feel.

> Nigel continued: "I feel increasingly annoyed each time you're late."

Step Five

Remember that all assertive communication is a two-way process, so it is important at this stage to ask for the other person's view, and how they think the situation could be improved. We need to recognise the value of working out a solution which suits both parties rather than imposing our own ideas on someone else.

> "Alison, why is this happening, and how do you think we can sort this out?" Alison explained that her husband had recently left her, leaving her alone to cope with three children. She had to take them to the child minder's each day before coming to work. She suggested that she change her shift, in order to fit in with her new commitments. This solution suited them both.

Step Six

State what the outcome of their behaviour will be. If an agreement cannot be reached it is important to spell out the consequences, ensuring they are reasonable and that you are prepared to carry them out.

> If Alison and Nigel had *not* been able to work out a solution, it would have been important for Nigel to point out the consequences and say clearly what he wanted: "I'd like you to report to me every morning on time. If by the end of the week there's no improvement in your time-keeping, I will have to involve the personnel department."

Of course people do not always stick to the agreements they have made, but, having once broached the subject, it is much easier for you to raise the issue again if the situation deteriorates.

Step Seven

It may be helpful to summarise the points that you have agreed on before ending on a positive comment.

> "I'm sure that we'll be able to work better in the future, having sorted this out Alison, and I'm really pleased we've had this discussion. Thank you for your honesty."

Putting off giving criticism only prolongs the agony. We are far more likely to give it constructively if we deal with a situation assertively as soon as it arises. Criticism in the area of sexuality can be especially difficult. Some of the conflicts we experience with regard to our sexuality are discussed in the next chapter.

9 Sexuality

Introduction

An assertive approach to sexuality is especially helpful, as this potentially difficult subject is relevant to us all. There is an illusion in society today that, as the display of sexuality becomes increasingly overt, people will be more able to speak honestly about it. The reality is that we often feel too embarrassed and inhibited to even broach the subject — secrecy surrounds the whole area of sexuality. As therapists, we need to acknowledge that this reality may exist both for our clients and ourselves.

Our discomfort will be all too apparent if we feel uneasy about facilitating a sexuality session. Giving ourselves permission not to include sexuality as a distinct session is perfectly acceptable. However you will find that it is practically impossible to teach assertiveness without making reference to issues of sexuality, as they are ever-present. Saying 'No', stating our needs and challenging society's expectations of us are all relevant issues. Making sexuality a natural part of the entire course by encouraging discussion whenever the subject is broached is a gentle way of desensitising people to the topic. The aim of an assertiveness programme is to raise awareness of certain important issues. It is not the time or the place to go into great detail, but, by gently touching the surface, we are opening up a path for further exploration, if people choose to take it.

The following issues are the ones we find most relevant: society's messages; body image; sexism; sexuality versus sensuality.

Society's Messages

A useful way to consider the variety of messages about sexuality that we receive throughout our lives is to brainstorm them with your group. It is helpful to look at the way these messages differ for men and women on the table overleaf.

These are just some of the examples. There are many more. Assertiveness encourages us to believe in ourselves and follow our own feelings and inclinations, whether or not they fit in with society's stereotypes.

Vicky grew up with little information about sex. At home the subject was considered taboo and never mentioned. Consequently she felt anxious and

Men	Women
You have to be tough. Tenderness is weak.	You must make yourself attractive to the opposite sex.
You have to have lots of partners to prove your virility.	You must not sleep around or else you will be considered cheap.
You have to be physical rather than emotional.	You have less of a sex drive than men.
You have to 'perform' in order to be a man.	You must do your duty and oblige your partner.
You have to make the first move.	You should wait for the man to initiate.

embarrassed whenever the topic was brought up by her friends. Being part of an assertiveness group enabled her to begin to challenge this strong message of secrecy.

"This is the first time I've felt able to talk about sex openly. I've always believed that it was somehow wrong to discuss it with anyone. I'm sure I'll still feel embarrassed at times, but, by sharing my feelings with other women, I've learnt so much about myself and my sexuality."

It is important to appreciate the power of these messages and to recognise the effect they have on the roles we assume in our lives.

Body Image

Although the issue of body image has relevance for both women and men, in our experience it has a far more powerful effect on women. Images of women in the media generally project youthfulness, slenderness and beauty, all of which are associated with sexual attractiveness. They also convey the idea that women need to dress in certain ways in order to please men. Such images are so powerful that many women resort to constant dieting in an effort to match them. For some, this can be a continuous battle, resulting in a distorted image of their own body, and a destructive pattern of eating, as in anorexia and bulimia nervosa.

Jennifer was determined to be slim and had been dieting furiously for many years. No matter how slim she became, she always saw herself as fat. She lost more and more weight and was eventually diagnosed as anorexic. After her weight had stabilised, she received assertiveness training as part of her treatment programme. This was aimed at raising her self-esteem and challenging her distorted body image. Although it was helpful for Jennifer to understand how trying to conform to society's view of women had been a contributory factor to her problems, it took many months of therapy for her to begin to make positive changes.

In recent years the media has turned its attention to the male image, displaying the broad, muscular and sleek male body, projecting an image of virility. Discussing the power of these images and their potentially negative effects is an opportunity many men may not have been given before.

Assertiveness, with its emphasis on self-esteem, encourages us to feel good about who we are and the way we look, regardless of what others think.

Sexism

Sexism is endemic in our society. We often fail to recognise it, as it is so much a part of our lives. We are conditioned from birth; boys have blue nurseries, girls have pink; boys are given cars to play with, girls have dolls. In adulthood the theme persists; men do the dirty work around the house, women clean and iron. The mature women in the office may still be referred to as 'the girls', which lowers their status at a stroke. In much the same way, the term 'lads' can be patronising to the men it refers to.

Sexism also works on a more obvious level; wolf-whistles in the street, sexual discrimination at work and, in many situations, overt sexual harassment. Even very extreme forms of sexism are tolerated by our society, such as comedians' sexual innuendo, the 'page three girl', and pornography in all its forms. Challenging sexism at any level becomes much more possible as we learn to communicate assertively.

Richard was an active member of a local trade union, whose main task for the year was to increase promotional opportunities for women within their organisation. Every meeting included a report and discussion on the progress which was being made. Richard noticed that, during the meeting, some of the men would make sexist jokes about women. He felt increasingly uncomfortable and decided to challenge their sexism.

"I find this difficult to say, but it seems incongruous on the one hand to be talking about women's rights, and on the other to be denying them by using such sexist humour. I'd like to suggest that we avoid making any sexist jokes during these meetings. How do people feel about that?"

Some of the men thought that this was quite unnecessary and weren't prepared to agree. However, afterwards, Richard was approached by other members of the group, who had not recognised their own sexism and were grateful for the insight. When talking about this in the assertiveness group, Richard said: "I realise that not everyone will change their behaviour because of what I've said, but I feel really pleased with myself for listening to my feelings and stating my beliefs."

This example illustrates how assertiveness is not concerned with winning. There is no guarantee that we will always get what we have asked for. The important point to remember is the increase we feel in our own self-respect as a result of making our request.

Sexuality Versus Sensuality

These two terms are often used interchangeably, although they mean quite different things. The *Concise Oxford English Dictionary* defines **sexuality** as: 'Of sex, a sex, or the sexes; pertaining to relations between the sexes, especially with reference to mutual attraction and to gratification of resulting desires.' We would suggest that sexuality also encompasses the whole way that society sees us as sexual beings.

In contrast the definition of **sensuality** is: 'Of sense or sensation, of or depending on the senses only and not on the intellect or spirit.' Sensual pleasures include feeling the warmth of the sun on our skin, stroking a kitten's fur, and the scent of new-mown hay. However each of us will find different sensations pleasurable. Some of us enjoy our hair being stroked, whilst others find it positively unpleasant, and those of us with hay fever are unlikely to feel inspired by the scent of cut grass!

Discussing our sensual pleasures and preferences in the group enables us to appreciate our own sensuality and to feel more comfortable with it. There is a tendency to perceive it as self-indulgent and time-wasting, and we often fail to recognise our daily experiences as being sensual. Encouraging people to view sensuality as something they can enjoy every day can add an extra dimension of pleasure to their lives. Sensuality can be very much a part of sexual sharing and can heighten our pleasure. Asking for our sensual needs to be met can be a starting-point from which to assert ourselves sexually.

> Brenda's life was hectic. She had a job, three children and a husband who spent long periods of time away from home. She recognised her tendency to rush through life, allowing little time for enjoying her own sensuality. After role-playing in the group, she decided to talk to her husband and ask him to fulfil one of her sensual needs. She chose a time when they were alone and relaxed together.
>
> "David, I feel embarrassed talking about this, but I feel distanced from you when you've been away, and I'd like us to spend more time together alone."
>
> David looked puzzled; "But I'm always around at the weekends, what more do you want?"
>
> "I know that, and I really appreciate the time we spend together as a family, but I'd like us to make some time for ourselves."
>
> "So what would you like us to do, then?"
>
> "I'd like us to sit like this and just to hold each other and feel close; I really enjoy it when we cuddle."

By recognising this sensual need, and using her assertive skills, Brenda had enhanced her relationship with her husband, and begun to allow herself more time to enjoy the sensual pleasures in life.

Working With Clients

Many of the clients with whom we work will have similar experiences to our own. However clients with special needs often have limited opportunities for both sexual and sensual experiences, and as therapists it is important for us to be aware of this. As this area can be threatening for many people, it is useful to offer them the opportunity to desensitise themselves further. Reading books, attending courses or receiving counselling or group therapy are all possible means of obtaining further information and support. It is useful for therapists to have such information available for those on their course, and so we have made several recommendations in Appendix II.

Respecting a person's right to privacy in the area of sexuality is essential. It is not our job to pry into people's sex lives and habits. The whole atmosphere of the group needs to be relaxed and non-judgemental. It is vital that we do not make assumptions about a person's sexuality. Assuming that everyone is in a relationship, and that all relationships are heterosexual or monogamous, reveals our own prejudice. It is helpful to refer to a person's 'partner', rather than assuming the sex of their companion, or whether or not they are married.

All aspects of assertive communication are relevant to dealing with issues of sexuality. The skill of self-disclosure is especially valuable, since the subject itself can be so sensitive and stressful. By handling situations more assertively we are effectively raising our self-esteem and reducing our stress. In coming to accept our sexuality we can learn to recognise and meet our sexual and sensual needs and choose whether to challenge some of the negative conditioning that has affected us thus far in our own lives.

Deciding whether to take the assertive option in such situations is our choice — something which we discuss in more detail in the next chapter.

10 The Assertive Option

Introduction

Realising that we are all able to choose how we behave is very empowering. Assertiveness is all about being in control of ourselves and taking the initiative. When we are assertive we have a sense of power within. In this chapter we will be looking at what we mean by personal power and how we can use or abuse it.

As this will be the last session, the aim is to bring together all the information that has been learnt so far and suggest ways in which people can continue to develop their learning after the course has finished.

What is Power?

The word 'power' often has many negative connotations, so it is helpful to clarify what we mean by personal or assertive power. If you ask a group what the word power means, they will often offer ideas such as:

▶ Wealth
▶ Domination
▶ Authority
▶ Using force
▶ Abusing others
▶ Coercion and control
▶ Exploitation

These are all descriptions of oppressive power, and therefore it can be useful to look at the differences between power and oppression. Taking an abbreviated definition from the *Concise Oxford English Dictionary*, **power** is: 'The ability to do or act, a particular faculty of body or mind', whereas **oppression** is: 'Overwhelming with superior weight of numbers or irresistible power; lying heavy on, weighing down, governing tyrannically, keeping under control by coercion, subjecting to continual cruelty or injustice.' Reading these, we can see that the ideas commonly used to describe power are more appropriate as descriptions of oppressive behaviour. If power is purely our ability to do, think or feel then personal power involves us doing, thinking or feeling for ourselves.

When we behave *assertively* we have a sense of power within, a strength inside us, which enables us to function on equal terms with others. When we behave *aggressively*, either directly or indirectly, we are displaying power over others. This abuse of our power, where we put others down and manipulate a situation for our own gain, means that we are behaving unequally. When we behave *passively* we feel powerless. This is because we are actively giving away our power to others and are then left feeling helpless and inferior. As a result, our interactions with others are always on an unequal level. Being assertive involves constructive, honest and open use of our personal power, respecting the rights of ourselves and those around us.

Inappropriate Use of Power

This can be a complex idea to get across, but one we feel is really helpful to understand. By learning to identify our own and others' behaviour, we are able to see much more clearly the way in which we all abuse and misuse our power. Whoever we are and whatever roles we assume in our lives we have the potential to do this. To demonstrate our inappropriate use of power we have compiled the following examples.

Direct Aggression: Abusing Power

We abuse our power by punishing and abusing others, and controlling them by denying their rights. Examples:

▶ The parent who withdraws their love as a punishment for the child's unacceptable behaviour: "You're a wicked child, get out of my sight until you can behave properly."

▶ The husband who tries to put guilt onto his wife for his own illness: "The way you go on, you'll make me worse; the doctor says my heart's not strong, you know."

▶ The friend who is consistently late, and always expects others to wait for him: "I don't know what you're making such a fuss about. You should know me by now, I'm always late."

Indirect Aggression: Misusing Power

We misuse our power by taking excessive care of others, so that they are dependent on us, and by using emotional blackmail to control those we love. Examples:

▶ The woman who chooses to be at the beck and call of her elderly parents, so that she feels needed and they are prevented from being independent.

▶ The person who tries to control their partner through love, denying them the chance to be anything other than what they want them to be: "I love you as you are, never never change."

► The teenage child who uses emotional blackmail with her parents in order to get what she wants: "You're saying that Phil and I can't see each other, but what would happen if I was pregnant? Then we'd have to get married."

Passivity: Giving Away Power

We give away our power by always opting for approval, waiting for others to make our lives better, and by never taking the risk of confronting something we don't like. Examples:

► The person who avoids pointing out bad workmanship to someone working on their house for fear of losing their approval.
► The woman who waits to be rescued from an abusive relationship, instead of ending it herself.
► The staff member who does not confront their boss over unfair work practices, thinking it is not their place to challenge them.

Assertive Power

At this stage we find it really helpful to include the group's ideas about what assertive power means. Affirming this is a very positive way of summing up the overall concept of assertiveness. The assertive expression of power requires:

Honesty	rather than	Deceit
Clarity	rather than	Vagueness
Equality	rather than	Injustice
Acceptance	rather than	Denial
Empathy	rather than	Self-centredness
Compromise	rather than	Victory
Sharing feelings	rather than	Hiding feelings
A congruent message	rather than	A fragmented message

Setting limits	rather than	Being imposed upon
Taking responsibility	rather than	Blaming others
Being strong	rather than	Being a victim
Taking the initiative	rather than	Waiting to be rescued
Believing in ourselves	rather than	Depending on others' approval
Action	*rather than*	*Reaction*

Assertive behaviour means choosing *action* rather than *reaction* in our lives. When we behave passively or aggressively we are often reacting to our own negative thoughts and feelings, instead of thinking things through and choosing to deal appropriately with the situation.

Where do we go from Here?

Assertiveness training can have such a dramatic effect on people's lives that they are often reluctant to end their learning as the course comes to a close. We therefore devote part of this last session to looking at the ways people can continue to develop their understanding and experience of assertiveness, as we too share the belief in the importance of continued learning. We suggest you provide a list of book titles you can personally recommend, and/or a box of books which people can borrow. With some encouragement a group will often meet and continue to support each other, occasionally calling on the facilitator for guidance. It is also possible for two or three people from the group to get together to role-play individual situations.

If you are aware of further courses which are available in the area, put people in touch with them. This could be a chance for someone to integrate further into the community, away from the safety of the hospital or unit. We find it very helpful to provide a follow-up session six to ten weeks after the original course has finished. It is worth remembering that for some clients it will be difficult to absorb all the information contained in a full course, and for that reason you may need to repeat the course several months after the first one.

Assertiveness training demonstrates to people that it is possible to change. Developing insight into our own and others' behaviour means that we are far more able to make an informed choice about how we wish to behave. In some respects this knowledge is the ending of our innocence, as we will never be able to see ourselves and others in quite the same light again.

Our whole experience of learning and teaching assertiveness has been enriching and rewarding for us both. We hope that you have already started to benefit from the sharing of our ideas and philosophy, and will feel confident and excited about putting some of them into practice.

The next chapter contains information about the clinical application of assertiveness and your role in planning and facilitating a course.

ll Clinical Application

Introduction

This chapter concentrates on the practical application of the material from the last ten chapters. Its dual aims are to assist you to establish assertiveness training as part of your treatment programme and to give examples of the way an assertive approach can help you in your working environment.

Timing

In order to follow a full course as detailed in the previous chapters, you would need to allow approximately 20 hours; this provides adequate time for sharing, role-play and group exercises. Our session plans cover two hours, but it is possible to spread the material out over a larger number of sessions, and in longer or shorter periods of time. We would suggest that, at first, you may need to break down the ten sessions in this way, until you become more familiar with the material.

Selection and Referral

Where possible, we prefer people to choose for themselves to attend an assertiveness course, rather than being sent by another professional. We recognise that this may not always happen; it is important to remember, though, that we can only change ourselves, not others. Assertiveness involves taking risks, and the first one to take is choosing to come to the initial session.

Before commencing an assertiveness programme with a client, it is important to spend some time assessing their needs and abilities. Each client will work at a different pace; some will have more insight than others. If your aim is to run a group, you need to select people, as far as possible, according to their ability. For example, in the field of mental health, out-patients are often much more able to benefit from the programme than those on an acute admission ward. We would suggest that you need to think carefully before applying the material to those with a history of psychosis. Those with profound learning difficulties are another group for whom assertiveness can be inappropriate, owing to the severity of their communication disorders.

Before anyone joins an assertiveness group it is important that they are first interviewed by the facilitator to ascertain both their ability to benefit from the material and their suitability for group work.

Group Dynamics

There are many advantages to be gained from acquiring assertive skills in a group setting. One of the most therapeutic effects is the amount of sharing and identification with others' problems. The sharing of others' experiences sharpens the perception with which we view our own; members of a group can learn as much from each other as they can from their facilitator.

An important issue to consider is that of gender. The decision whether to run a mixed or single-sex group may not always be within your control, but in our experience single-sex groups are easier. However, if you have a co-worker of the opposite sex, it can be a positive advantage to run a mixed group, as each sex has its own role model to learn from.

We suggest that 12 people is the maximum number for a group run by one therapist, the minimum being six and the optimum nine. This will inevitably depend on the ability of the group. Below six, the group becomes too intensive; above 12 and there is little opportunity for the therapist to facilitate individual role-plays.

There are occasions when it is not possible or appropriate for clients to work in a group, and in these cases we have adapted the assertiveness programme to individual sessions. Indications for individual work:

▶ there is no appropriate group available;
▶ the client is afraid of working with others;
▶ the pace at which the client absorbs ideas would be markedly slower than the rest of the group;
▶ the client is too demanding for groupwork.

There are, however, two main limitations in individual work: role-play is restricted and can never be truly effective; and clients miss out on shared experiences and the chance to identify with others who have similar problems to their own. Individual work can be an essential first stage for some people, affording them the opportunity to explore different ideas and to practise new behaviours in the safety of a one-to-one situation. The confidence gained from this will often result in a client feeling able to continue their learning within a group.

Facilitator's Role

We have really struggled to find a word other than 'teaching' to describe how we pass on the principles of assertiveness. We like to think of ourselves as 'facilitating' our clients learning, rather than feeding them the information in a rote fashion. Hence the large experiential component in the exercises. We hope that you will see the importance of this, should you choose to undertake a course yourself. It is worth remembering that you will be acting as an assertive role model for your clients, and therefore it is essential that you are aware of your own behaviour and are prepared to share your own experiences, both positive and negative.

We have shared with our clients the times when we have resorted to passive or aggressive behaviour, as well as those when we have been assertive. It is very common for people to see the facilitator as an assertiveness 'guru': someone who never fails to say 'No', always states their needs and can cope with criticism without flinching. They often imagine that our self-esteem is indestructible. There are dangers in succumbing to this tempting image; the best way of avoiding this is to share honestly from your own experience.

If you have the chance to work with another trainer, take it; you will undoubtedly benefit from having the practical and emotional support of your colleague, and the group members will have the advantage of two points of view.

Client Groups

Our main experience of using assertiveness as a treatment method has been with the following four groups:

▶ People with learning difficulties
▶ People who feel depressed and anxious
▶ People who stammer
▶ People with problem eating patterns

Many of the aims of treatment with these client groups will be the same. We have listed those common to all clients below:

▶ increasing self-awareness;
▶ learning strategies for changing behaviour;
▶ developing effective communication skills;
▶ raising self-esteem;
▶ encouraging the honest expression of feelings;
▶ coping with stressful situations;
▶ building self-confidence;
▶ taking responsibility for their life.

More specific advantages of assertiveness training are listed under each client group.

People With Learning Difficulties

Using assertiveness with this client group can be immensely rewarding, for facilitator and client alike. Obviously those whose difficulties are profound will be unable to participate in this type of approach, but for those with less severe handicaps the material can be adapted and presented in smaller sections over a longer period of time.

Assertiveness fits in readily with the current move towards total advocacy for people with learning difficulties. The closure of large institutions, resulting in resettlement in the community, has made it more necessary than ever for these clients to develop their interpersonal and communication skills.

When clients' general communication skills are at a low level it may be necessary for the group to work on listening skills and turn-taking in conversation before starting on an assertiveness programme. Confidence in speaking in front of a group develops slowly, therefore it is important that group sessions last for at least an hour, preferably two, to allow people plenty of time to relax and participate. The ideal session lasts two hours, with a half-hour break in the middle, and the presentation of information and activities needs to be varied to take account of limited periods of concentration and different levels of literacy. If the group has previous experience of using video and are comfortable with it, it can be a helpful tool when learning about different behaviour types and looking at body language.

The ratio of therapists to clients needs to be higher in direct relation to the level of skill of the group, with a recommended minimum of one therapist to six clients. If the group has a low or mixed level of skills, then two to eight is recommended; this ensures adequate support in role-play, which would be conducted in pairs, with the therapist observing.

It is vital, with this group of clients, that their main carers are involved in the work that is being undertaken, otherwise they could remain unaware of, and resistant to, the clients' reasons for wanting to change their behaviour. The issue of 'rights' is central to every assertiveness group, but it is of paramount importance to people with learning difficulties. These people's rights are so often abused, sometimes by the very people who, with the best will in the world, are trying to care for them. The most positive way of involving carers is to have them join in with an assertiveness group, as this ensures a mutual understanding and acceptance of the individual's aims.

This group of clients often have the ability to recall events, but lack the skill to discuss the feelings evoked by them. This situation is due in part to the fact that they do not have the words in their vocabulary to describe how they feel. Devoting time to developing the skill of self-disclosure forms an important part of any assertiveness course. Time should be given to the safe expression of anger, a feeling which, traditionally, those with learning difficulties have rarely been encouraged to express.

Advantages for this client group are:

▶ improved interpersonal skills;
▶ learning how to talk about feelings;
▶ recognition of their 'rights';
▶ development of confidence in their own communication ability.

Case history

Grant attended the assertiveness group because all his friends from the club were taking part. He lived in a small group home and was employed in a sheltered workshop. The group consisted of both carers and clients.

At the start of the assertiveness course Grant was very passive, speaking so quietly that he was difficult to hear, even when the dominant group members were quiet. His body was always moving, hands rubbing his legs, rocking to and fro, twitching, and his eyes were rarely raised from the carpet.

Change began when the group agreed to respect each other's space and to speak in turn. Grant began to take his own space to speak his mind, without being interrupted by other members who, until now, had given him constant put-downs. The session on body language had a dramatic impact; he raised his shoulders and made eye contact, at first only fleetingly. Over a period of weeks he grew in confidence and self-esteem, showing leadership skills within the group by encouraging a return to work after coffee breaks and reminding others to allow quieter members their space. Grant's membership and contributions began to be appreciated by the whole group.

At the end of the 12-week course he asked for duplicate sets of handouts and support in sharing his new skills with other residents at his home. Grant began for the first time in his life to see himself as equal to others, recognising that, whilst he was not attaining all his goals, he was growing in confidence and self-esteem each time he took a risk and acted assertively.

People Who Feel Depressed and Anxious

Those readers working in the mental health field will appreciate that an individual's problems may often encompass many different aspects of their lives. Feelings of depression and anxiety are often an expression of unresolved issues from past experiences or present circumstances. It is therefore necessary to give space within a group or individual session for people to look at such issues as and when they arise. This means that you need to be flexible in the way you run the group or facilitate the individual session.

Another factor to consider is the style in which you, as a therapist, generally work. Assertiveness, as we have said, is predominantly a behavioural approach, rather than psychodynamic, so you may need to make it clear both to clients and referring agents that the work will be taking on a behavioural slant.

Working with clients with acute difficulties may be a long-term process; a client will not necessarily be enabled to make changes in their life after an initial course in assertiveness. Progress in this area will naturally be determined by the client's motivation to change, and the pace at which they can work with the material. Working with a client on an out-patient basis will often be far more effective than struggling to help them during their acute crisis. Providing follow-up work can also be helpful in facilitating the client towards further change and progress after their initial course of treatment.

Assertiveness is also relevant to clients with long-term needs, but the material may have to be adapted, with shorter sessions being used to allow for reduced concentration levels. Role-plays need to be specific to clients' needs and experiences, especially if they are institutionalised. Much of the information in the above section on those with learning difficulties is also relevant for this group of clients.

Most of us recognise that our own self-esteem is lowered when we feel anxious or depressed, so strategies for building self-esteem are especially relevant for this group. It is important to acknowledge that the lowered level of their self-esteem is directly linked to the depth of their depression.

People need an insight into their own problems and behaviour patterns before they can apply any of the learning from an assertiveness programme. Those who are in acute crisis, or who have expressed suicidal thoughts, may possibly benefit more in the first instance from direct support and care, than from participating in a full programme. Learning to be more assertive is often a goal cited by many who wish to overcome their difficulties, but the introduction of this needs to be well timed.

Advantages for this client group are:

▶ becoming more in touch with their feelings;
▶ overcoming fears;
▶ working on presenting issues with new insight;
▶ developing positive thinking patterns;
▶ learning to take control of their lives.

Case history

Tom was 28 when he was admitted to the acute ward of a psychiatric hospital. He had attempted suicide on two occasions prior to his admission, and was very depressed and anxious. He was referred for individual assertiveness training, as it was felt he was particularly unassertive in his behaviour, and had a severe loss of self-esteem.

After an initial assessment it was agreed to commence individual therapy and review his progress at 12-week intervals. Tom was seen twice weekly for six weeks, during which time he was discharged from hospital. He then attended weekly out-patient sessions for a further year. It was explained to him that, whilst assertiveness training would form part of his therapy, time would also be given for him to work on current unresolved issues. A weekly assertiveness programme was not followed; instead the information was given throughout the year's therapy. Tom used the sessions to resolve current issues by working out assertive strategies for coping.

In the first two months he began to acknowledge his passivity and how his suicide attempts related to that behaviour, but had difficulty at this stage in acknowledging his aggression. The next five months' work centred on enabling Tom to become more in touch with his feelings and looked at his difficulty with self-disclosure and stating his needs. He felt pressurised and conditioned by society not to express his feelings openly because he was a man.

During the year's therapy, Tom attempted suicide twice. The first occasion was approximately two weeks after discharge, the second after eight months of therapy. Tom recognised that the first attempt was a demonstration of his passivity in an extreme sense, and he acknowledged his responsibility for his behaviour. The second attempt was a spontaneous reaction to the enormous despair he felt at the depth of his feelings, and was a much more serious attempt. In the months that followed, Tom began to challenge his depressive feelings with great vigour. The most significant change was his recognition of his passivity, the result of which was a reduction in the frequency of his depressive bouts, and a considered decision not to attempt suicide again.

During therapy Tom attended college and took up various hobbies. He began to build friendships with women, something he had previously been scared of doing.

In the last session Tom described how he felt it was now up to him to make something of his life and that when he became depressed he would need to deal with it, rather than 'wallow' in it. With this attitude he decided to terminate the therapy.

People Who Stammer

In many communication exchanges the stammerer is bound to think of themselves as unequal. Assertiveness develops the skills of thinking equally, as well as acting equally. Assertive thought encourages stammerers to replace the negative thoughts they have about themselves with positive ones. Thus "I'll never get this sentence out, I'm hopeless at this" becomes "It may take some time, but I can do it. I'm not hopeless, I've got lots of skills in dealing with people."

Learning assertive skills encourages stammerers to put effort into the non-verbal as well as the verbal aspects of their message, helping them to develop into more effective communicators. Their self-esteem develops in proportion to their increasing skills, leading to greater self-confidence when speaking is involved.

Learning about the 'rights' is a voyage of discovery for many clients. For people who stammer, the right to make a mistake and still be treated with respect has a special significance. Many hold the belief that fluency is perfection, and stammers are mistakes to be avoided at all costs. Using the skill of self-disclosure can have a liberating effect, encouraging the acknowledgement and expression of feelings which have been buried deeply for many years. This can be facilitated by allowing plenty of time for people to share the way they feel within the group.

Group therapy with people who stammer is a well accepted method of treatment. Therefore this can be one of the easiest places to begin using assertiveness. If there is an established group for stammerers it is often possible to use ten weeks of the group's programme to cover the topic of assertiveness.

When establishing the guidelines for this group, be aware of the need to discuss the issue of fluency techniques. If individual members want to use their time in the group to practise a particular fluency technique then that is their decision and sole responsibility, not the focus of the group or the therapist. It is not surprising that stammerers focus on their fluency when selecting role-plays. Encourage the selection of situations that focus on what they have said rather than how they have said it.

Naturally people who stammer are anxious to know whether assertiveness will increase their fluency. Our results have shown that this is very often the case, but there is no guarantee that it will have that effect immediately, and people may still find themselves feeling unequal when communicating with fluent speakers. However, as the twin concepts of assertive thought and assertive action begin to take effect, fluency often increases.

Advantages for this client group are:

▶ reducing the stress felt in any communication exchange;

▶ emphasising the importance of the non-verbal aspects of communication;

▶ encouraging the use of self-disclosure, especially in the area of non-fluency;

▶ having permission not to have 'perfect' speech all the time.

Case history

Henry was 21 when he first came for speech therapy. He arrived for the initial appointment with his mother, who was his constant companion. His self-esteem was at rock bottom. He described how he had neither a job nor friends nor any contact outside his own family.

His overt stammer was slight, but he expended most of his energy on keeping it hidden, which only served to increase his sensitivity and anxiety.

He began therapy by having twice-weekly individual treatment using block modification, and after two months he had gained enough confidence to join a group. Initially he worked on conventional stammering therapy, but after three months expressed a desire to join an assertiveness group for stammerers. The effect of the group was immediate and positive. He was able to recognise his former behaviour as passive and self-defeating. He realised that he had been sitting at home waiting for things to get better: a job to magically appear, his stammer to go away.

The assertive message about taking responsibility for making things happen in his life encouraged him to apply for jobs. He eventually found one that he enjoyed. He left home, found his own flat and gradually made friends with people of his own age. His preoccupation with his stammer faded. As he said, "I'm much more concerned with what I'm saying now, rather than with how I'm saying it."

People With Problem Eating Patterns

Anorexia and bulimia generally share the themes of low self-esteem and poor body image. Most of the information in the section on depression and anxiety is also applicable for this client group. However an additional factor which needs to be considered is the effect of too much task-orientated input on clients with these problems. Each therapist has their own approach, but setting homework tasks or goals relating to the assertiveness programme may be destructive, as this can often bring up issues of control and fear of failing, and so encourage the pattern of secrecy and deception.

It may be helpful to spend a considerable period of time working on the twin issues of body image and society's unrealistic expectations, both of which affect self-esteem, as these are common components of any eating disorder. Working with clients in relation to their sexuality and sensual expression may also need emphasis; there is much research to suggest that problems with sexuality are intrinsically linked to disruptive eating patterns.

Clients who present with such difficulties are often very defensive and may block attempts made to facilitate personal change. It may be worthwhile addressing this issue at an initial interview, not only to check out motivation, but also to look at the reasons for denial or resistance and the secondary gains for this type of behaviour. A confrontational approach may be required in order to encourage a client to be responsible for making their own decisions about using the material.

The advantages for this type of client group are as follows:

▶ exploring society's expectations in relation to body image;

▶ taking responsibility for their own eating behaviour;

▶ enabling assertive expression of sexual and sensual needs;

▶ confronting secrecy and deception by being honest with themselves and others.

Case history

Fiona was a young woman of 20, who had been referred for individual work by her general practitioner. An initial assessment revealed that her eating pattern had been distorted for approximately seven years, and the overriding issue was her suppression of any sexual or sensual expression. Fiona said at her first session that she believed her eating and sexual problems were too much of a coincidence not be related. Her self-image was very poor and she showed little confidence in her abilities.

Fiona was permanently weight-conscious and her whole day revolved around food. Her initial pattern had been typically anorexic, maintaining a daily 600–800 calorie diet. However in the last year she had used 'binging' and vomiting as a means of taking in a higher calorific food content. She had only begun to use laxatives in the last few months, when she did not feel she had enough privacy to vomit.

As Fiona developed trust in the therapist, she began to discuss her difficulty in saying 'No', and her predominantly passive behaviour pattern. Stating her needs, or how she felt, was something she found difficult. This was a particular problem for her when she did not want to be caressed or touched by her boyfriend, but was unable to tell him how she felt.

The weekly sessions concentrated on enabling Fiona to understand her behaviour and engage in using assertive skills to overcome her passivity. As she had a tendency to set herself up for failure by taking on situations which she could not handle confidently, Fiona began learning to say 'No' using graded examples from her everyday life. It took many sessions before she was able to look at being assertive in sexual situations with her boyfriend.

Space was given in the sessions to looking at the way Fiona felt pressurised to conform to certain expectations, including an ideal body image. She acknowledged that she tended to give up if she did not achieve the ideal goal, which was often related to her weight, and would then become depressed as a result. This was a pattern she was able to change to some degree by thinking in a more positive way about her life and her abilities.

Emphasis was given to the aspect of honesty in assertive communication, as there was so much secrecy attached to her problem. Fiona gradually began to share her fear of putting on weight and her disturbed eating patterns with friends and family. Learning the skill of self-disclosure made some significant changes for her in relationships, especially with her boyfriend.

Fiona was seen for a total of five months. Her level of self-esteem increased significantly and she began to communicate more assertively. She became less weight-conscious and more relaxed about her eating; she had some difficulty, however, in letting go of her pattern of dieting altogether. Fiona decided to continue working by herself on her problems and agreed to contact the therapist if she wanted further sessions.

An Account of a Group

We have detailed above four case histories of individuals who have had assertiveness training as part of a treatment programme. We thought it would be useful at this point to give an account of a group which incorporates assertiveness, concentrating on the group process rather than the clients' progress. With certain client groups it will be appropriate to use a straightforward assertiveness training package, as detailed in Appendix I. Clients such as groups of stammerers, or those with learning difficulties, are most likely to benefit from this straightforward application. In the mental health field, it is not always easy to run an 'Assertiveness Group', nor is it necessarily the most effective way of enabling clients' growth. This is particularly relevant for clients whose concentration on learning and changing may be impaired by the depth of their feeling.

Some of the difficulties of using a structured approach in the mental health field are outlined here:

▶ Clients are often too anxious to concentrate well on a detailed training programme;

▶ Clients may become upset, angry or tearful and need time and space to work on the personal issue that has arisen, rather than learn about assertiveness;

▶ It may be necessary to look at the group dynamics, especially if it is an on-going psychotherapeutic group, rather than centre on direct learning;

▶ The group may feel disempowered by a therapist who changes role from 'counsellor' to 'teacher';

▶ Clients may not feel confident enough to undertake role-play on request;

▶ Clients may lack a sense of control and find it difficult to accept responsibility for their own change.

All these factors become areas of concern if you run a group as an assertiveness training course. We give below an example of how an on-going awareness group, for clients attending a unit on a daily basis, incorporated the assertiveness package over a number of months.

The open group usually consisted of ten clients, two students and two therapists. It was entitled an 'awareness group', the main aim being to increase self-awareness and enable personal change to occur. A variety of techniques were used, including games, exercises, teaching sessions, use of video, role-play, sociodrama exercises, writing and discussion.

The clients were mixed as to sex, age and ability. Each client had their own personal issues to confront, but there were shared themes of low self-esteem, lack of trust, being stuck in negative behaviour patterns and feeling unable to change. Over a period of several months, the group looked at different ways of developing their self-awareness, using the concept of transactional analysis, family dynamics and the video. When the themes in the group related to assertiveness, the following aspects were worked on:

▶ Behaviour types

▶ Rights

▶ Self-disclosure

▶ Skills

▶ Criticism and conflict

The information was not taught, rather gathered from the group as a means of empowering each client.

As an example, in order to look at behaviour types, the group opted to divide into four smaller groups each brainstorming a behaviour type. Feeding back afterwards enabled them to identify commonly used behaviour and what each individual wished to change. The latter part of the two-hour session used role-play in small groups to work on particular situations.

At another time the issue of confrontation was raised by the group. One member wished to learn how to handle her husband's constant put-downs, and consequently the session centred on ways of dealing with conflict assertively.

Running a group with a more flexible approach requires an openness on the part of the facilitator and a willingness to work with whatever issues the group raises. This process enables clients to work at their own pace, and to make their own choices and decisions.

We cannot stress too strongly that the above account is based on our experience in mental health. Normally, when you run an assertiveness course with any client, whether individually or in a group, it is important to recognise that their primary problem could dominate the course content. While it may be important to deal with whatever the client raises in this situation, it needs to be made clear at the outset that the main aim is to improve their assertiveness.

Using Assertiveness in the Working Environment

Clients often give examples of their difficulties in being assertive with their professional carers. We find it frustrating, knowing that, if the professionals were willing to learn how to be more assertive themselves, they would be enabling their clients to be more assertive. What is encouraging is that we receive an increasing number of requests to run training courses from our own and related professions. We feel this is a very positive step, acknowledging as it does the value of working together in a more open, honest and equal environment. Those of us working within the public sector, especially in the field of education and health, are used to a hierarchical system: one which acknowledges very clearly that the consultant is apparently more important than the student nurse, the headmistress more important than the school caretaker, and certainly that the therapist is more important than the client.

One advantage of adopting an assertive approach to working together is the emphasis on team-building, which results in people recognising and valuing their own skills. Assertiveness teaches equality and respect, virtues which are often lacking in hierarchical organisations. As increased self-esteem results in a feeling of internal power, people become more able to confront behaviour they are uncomfortable with, from whichever direction it may come.

Mac was a speech therapist working in a stroke unit. At the monthly case discussion on one of his patients the consultant was suggesting that there was little that could be done to help with his severe swallowing difficulties. Mac held a different view, and knew that using an assertive approach would help him to put over his point of view.

Donald: Right then — that's all we need to say about Mr Allen; we'll review his progress again in three months' time.

Mac: I want to say something else, Donald, before we move on to the next patient. I'd really like to try out a palatal training appliance with Mr Allen, as I've had some excellent results with them in the past. What I need is for you to refer him to Oral Surgery.

Donald: Oh I don't think so, it would just be a waste of time. Oral Surgery is a very busy department. I don't think we should bother them with this.

Mac: I realise Oral Surgery is over-stretched, Donald, and I wouldn't suggest this unless I was confident that it had a good chance of success.

Donald: How can you be so sure? I've had a lot of experience with these types of patients and in my opinion we'd just be raising false hopes.

Mac: I recognise your experience in the field, Donald; however I too have specialised experience in this particular area, which leads me to believe that a PTA would be appropriate.

Donald: Well all right, Mac, we'll give it a try, but I want to review him after six months to see how it's going.

Mac: That sounds fine to me. I'll make sure you have the anemometry results and an up-to-date report in good time for the next meeting. Thanks for your help, I really appreciate it.

Confronting someone we perceive to be of higher status will usually provoke a greater degree of anxiety. There is a risk that our body language will reveal this tension. If we read Mac's responses above in a hard, sharp voice, we can see how important it is to pay attention to the pace and tone of our voice in order to be assertive and not to be aggressive. In our class-conscious society we are unused to being challenged by those whom we perceive to be of lower status. This is why great care has to be taken when being assertive in these situations, in order that we are not misinterpreted.

The example above is just one of the positive results of a professional having assertiveness training. 'Assertiveness breeds assertiveness' and this is especially true within teams who have taken the risk of doing assertiveness training together. The fear of exposing our weaknesses to our colleagues is a genuine concern, particularly at the beginning of the course, but one which is easily dispelled by the non-judgemental nature of the training.

Learning that conflict is inevitable within any group of people, and that it can be handled without penalties on either side, is immensely empowering. When this openness and honesty is shared with our clients there is no end to what we can achieve together.

The rewards of assertive communication are so tangible; the effects are immediate and life-enhancing. All of us, clients and therapists alike, are already assertive at many times in our lives. The value of assertiveness training is that it greatly increases the chances of our choosing the assertive option more often.

APPENDIX I <u>Session Plans</u>

There are a number of basic considerations to take into account before setting up your group.

<u>VENUE</u>

▶ The venue you choose is important
▶ Aim to provide a warm, comfortable environment which ensures privacy.
▶ The room must be large enough to allow work in small groups.
▶ The chairs need to be comfortable and easily moved.
▶ It helps to have a clock in a prominent position.
▶ Keeping to your programme times is made easier if there is easy access to tea- and coffee-making facilities.

<u>TIMING</u>

These session plans are presented as a guide for running your own groups. There is a great deal of information to cover in each session, and as a result there can be a dilemma between the time given to presentation of the material and the time given to group discussion. However it is important to bear in mind that the timings given are only a guideline and that the following plans can be used flexibly.

SESSION ONE

Handouts: A   *Introduction to Assertiveness*
               B   *Book List*
Exercises: Name Game
               Group Rules
               Hopes and Fears
Equipment: Flipchart, pens and paper

Content	Time in minutes
Welcome. Introduce yourself as facilitator. Supply environmental information, eg. toilets, fire escape. Explain your role as enabler, rather than teacher. Describe the format of the course, including length and number of sessions.	15
Name Game Exercise	10
Group Rules Exercise Include confidentiality, punctuality, smoking, using 'I' statements.	10
Hopes and Fears Exercise	10
Feedback	15
Break	15
Explain techniques used during the course: brainstorming, feedback and role-play.	10
Brainstorm the definition of assertiveness. Clarify the difference between assertiveness and aggression.	10
Discuss Handout A, with emphasis on personal change and the importance of sharing this with family and friends.	10
Ask participants to consider behaviours they would like to change. Work in pairs.	10
Distribute Handout B.	
Closing exercise: share with the group something enjoyed in the session.	5

HANDOUT A *Introduction to Assertiveness*

Assertiveness is:

▶ The ability to express our ideas and feelings, both positive and negative, in an open, direct and honest manner.

▶ The ability to stand up for our rights, while respecting the rights of others.

▶ The ability to take responsibility for ourselves and our actions, without judging or blaming other people.

▶ The ability to find a compromise where conflict exists.

All of us behave assertively at times, but when we feel vulnerable or unsure we may resort to using aggressive, manipulative or passive behaviour.

Assertiveness training increases the chances of our using assertive behaviour more often, especially when we most need to.

Learning the skills of assertiveness enables us to change our old patterns of behaviour and to develop a more positive approach to life.

Changing the way we respond to others can be exciting and stimulating. It is important to share these changes with those close to us, as this helps them to feel included, rather than threatened by the changes.

This course provides the opportunity to develop self-awareness and insight into your own and others' behaviour, in a supportive and caring environment.

HANDOUT B *Book List*

The books listed below are ones you may find helpful to increase your understanding of assertiveness.

Author	Title	Publisher
Alberti & Emmons	*Your Perfect Right*	Impact
Back, Ken & Kate	*Assertiveness at Work*	McGraw-Hill
Butler, Pam	*Self-Assertion for Women*	Harper & Row
Dickson, Anne	*A Woman in Your Own Right*	Quartet
Hare, Beverley	*Be Assertive*	Optima
Lindenfield, Gael	*Assert Yourself*	Thorsons
Phelps & Austin	*The Assertive Woman*	Impact

The following titles are useful for developing our self-awareness.

Allen, Yvonne	*Successfully Single, Successfully Yourself*	Cedar
Cleese & Skynner	*Families and How to Survive Them*	Methuen
Harris, Thomas	*I'm OK, You're OK*	Pan
Jeffers, Susan	*Feel The Fear and Do It Anyway*	Century
Norwood, Robin	*Women Who Love too Much*	Arrow
Orbach & Eichenbaum	*What do Women Want?*	Pelican
Orbach & Eichenbaum	*Bitter Sweet*	Pelican

SESSION ONE   Exercises

Name Games

Here are three examples to choose from:

1 Ask the group to arrange themselves in a circle in alphabetical order of their first names, then go round the circle saying their name.

2 Ask each member of the group to share their name and explain what they know about its origin.

3 Each member thinks of a positive adjective that begins with the same sound as their first name, eg. Bouncy Brenda, Kind Karl, and shares it with the group.

Group Rules

Form into groups of four and ask people to consider what rules they would like the group to follow throughout the course. Feed back the results and record on flipchart. Display the rules for the first few sessions as a reminder. Ensure that the points mentioned on the session plan are included.

Hopes and Fears

Ask the group to get into pairs and share their hopes and fears about the course, taking five minutes each. Where possible, encourage people to work with someone they do not already know. Feed back to the group. This will illustrate that people have many of the same hopes and fears.

SESSION TWO

Handouts: C *Behaviour Types*
D *Identification of Different Behaviours*
E *Personal Programme*

Exercises: Brainstorm Behaviour Types
Demonstration of Behaviour Types
Identification of Different Behaviours
Personal Programmes

Equipment: Flipchart, pens and paper

Content	Time in minutes
Sharing and feedback: working in pairs, share experiences, both positive and negative, since the last session. Each participant to feed back one positive and one negative to the whole group. Facilitator to encourage learning from the negative.	15
Brainstorm Behaviour Types Exercise	10
Feedback	10
Demonstration of Behaviour Types Exercise Discussion of points raised Distribute Handout C.	15
Break	15
Identification of Different Behaviours Exercise Distribute Handout D. Feed back results to whole group. Facilitator to clarify any confusion.	15 15
Explain Personal Programmes. Emphasise the need for a hierarchy, and being specific. Tell the group that a situation can be something they have already done or something they would like to do.	10
Distribute Handout E. Ask participants to fill in at least one situation, in the group, and to complete it before next week's session.	10
Closing exercise: share with the group a feeling that they have at that moment.	5

HANDOUT C *Behaviour Types*

DIRECT AGGRESSION

**BOSSY
ARROGANT
BULLDOZING
INTOLERANT
OPINIONATED
OVER-BEARING**

INDIRECT AGGRESSION

**SARCASTIC
DECEIVING
AMBIGUOUS
INSINUATING
MANIPULATIVE
GUILT INDUCING**

PASSIVITY

**WAITING
MOANING
HELPLESS
SUBMISSIVE
INDECISIVE
APOLOGETIC**

ASSERTIVENESS

**DIRECT
HONEST
POSITIVE
ACCEPTING
RESPONSIBLE
SPONTANEOUS**

HANDOUT D *Identification of Different Behaviours*

	Situation	Response	Behaviour
1	A neighbour calls at your house to ask you to help with the school fair.	"I'd like to help you with the fair, but I'm not sure if I'm free then. I'll get back to you tomorrow."	
2	You arrange to meet a friend for a meal. He is half an hour late, but full of apologies.	"Oh good, you're here at last. I'm absolutely starving; I didn't get time for lunch today, but it doesn't matter."	
3	The television repairer promises to return the following day with your television. When he doesn't, you ring the shop to complain.	"I'm fed up with your awful service — I won't buy anything from you ever again!"	
4	You are served a cold cup of tea in a cafe.	You say nothing to the waitress but pull a face when you drink the tea.	
5	Your friend telephones you and chats for a long time. You would like to finish the conversation.	"I'm ever so sorry, but I'm going to have to go: the cat's just been sick and the children are shouting for their tea. I'm really sorry. I hope you don't mind."	
6	A meeting is being planned to arrange a Christmas party. The time suggested is not convenient for you.	"I'd like to come to the meeting, but unfortunately I won't be able to. Please would you give my apologies and ensure that I'm sent the minutes?"	
7	You live in a shared house. The person whose room is next to yours plays loud music well into the night.	You bang on the wall, shouting: "Will you stop that dreadful row, I'm sick to death of it!"	
8	You go to buy a pair of shoes. The salesman is very pushy and says, 'I think these are perfect for you', but you are not convinced.	"Well, I'm not really sure, but if you think they look nice, I'll have them."	

	Situation	Response	Behaviour
9	Your parents telephone to invite you to a party they are giving for their friends. You are uncomfortable with most of the people invited and do not want to go.	In a sarcastic tone: "It sounds like a whole lot of fun — just what I need after a hard week in the office. I suppose you'd be upset if I didn't come."	
10	The barmaid serves you the wrong drink in the pub.	"What do you call this? I asked for a shandy, not lager — get your act together, love."	
11	You are feeling put upon at work and decide to ask for a rise.	"I'd like to talk about my pay with you. Please could we meet next week to discuss it further?"	
12	You ask your friend to look after your dog for the weekend, while you visit your sick aunt.	"I know I can rely on you to look after Rover for me this weekend. I couldn't possibly not visit Aunt Jane and there's no one else I could ask."	
13	Your teenage child has left her bedroom in a complete mess.	"I feel angry when you leave your clothes all over the floor, Ros; I'd like you to tidy it up before the weekend."	
14	A new colleague, with whom you share an office, smokes continuously. You dislike the smell of smoke.	"Gosh, I've really got a headache, but then smoky atmospheres always bring on my migraine."	
15	Your partner is obviously upset about something, but doesn't discuss it with you.	"What the hell's wrong with you, sitting there sulking all evening?"	
16	A friend has borrowed money from you several times and not repaid it. She asks again.	"Er, um, well actually, . . . that's OK, I think. Um, how much would you like?"	

HANDOUT E *Personal Programme*

No	Person	Situation	Feelings	Desired Assertive Behaviour
eg.	My friend Alison	She was late last night when we'd arranged to go out for the evening	Frustrated and anxious about saying anything	To ask her not to be late again when we have arranged to go out together
1				
2				
3				
4				
5				

Select a situation which you feel you can almost handle assertively and write it as number one. Arrange the rest in order of difficulty down to number five. Therefore the most difficult situation will be number five, the easiest number one.

SESSION TWO   Exercises

Brainstorm Behaviour Types

Prepare four large sheets of paper, each one headed with a different behaviour type. Write a few words on each, describing the behaviour, as a prompter. Divide the group into four and give each group a sheet. Ask them to write down all the words and phrases they can think of which describe that behaviour. Feed back the results in a large group and display the sheets.

Demonstration of Behaviour Types

The aim of this exercise is to demonstrate the effect of our behaviour on others. The facilitator demonstrates each behaviour type with a volunteer from the group, using one example throughout: eg. requesting a fresh cup of coffee, or using a simple example given by the group. The volunteers' role is to listen to the facilitator; stress that they do not have to reply. The facilitator demonstrates each behaviour in turn: eg. 'Er, excuse me waiter, I'm terribly sorry to bother you, but I think this coffee is a bit cold. I don't suppose it would be possible to have a fresh cup, would it?'

Ask the volunteers to return to their seat to think about how they would feel. Repeat this exercise for all four behaviours, finishing on assertiveness. Ask the volunteers in turn to share with the group how they felt on the receiving end. Examples:

Passivity — frustration, annoyance.

Indirect aggression — guilt, confusion.

Direct aggression — humiliation, embarrassment.

Assertiveness — respect, acknowledgement.

Elicit from the group the difference between assertion and other behaviours: eg. shorter, specific, more effective, respects the other person.

Identification of Different Behaviours

Distribute Handout D. Ask participants to read all the examples and identify in the right-hand column which behaviour is being used.

Key to Handout D

Passivity	4	5	8	16
Indirect aggression	2	9	12	14
Direct aggression	3	7	10	15
Assertion	1	6	11	13

Personal Programmes

In order to decide which situations to role-play, group members need to write their own personal programmes. Ask them to think of five situations they would like to deal with more assertively and list them on Handout E, numbered according to their difficulty. Emphasise the following points:

▶ Situations can be either something they have already done or something they would like to do.

▶ Situations need to be specific: eg. 'Coping with my partner' would need to be made clearer, as in 'Asking my partner not to smoke in the bedroom.'

▶ Situations with friends or partners that have a long history are usually more difficult than those with people we do not know well.

▶ Situations need to range from the simplest to the most difficult.

SESSION THREE

Handouts: F   *Body Language*
                    G   *The Toolkit*
                    H   *Role-play*

Exercises: Body Language and Behaviour Types
                    Demonstration of Skills
                    Demonstration Role-play

Equipment: Flipchart and pens, large poster illustrating toolkit

Content	Time in minutes
Sharing and Feedback	15
Introduce concept of body language; emphasise that at least 75 per cent of communication is non-verbal; assertion means matching non-verbal with verbal; message needs to be clear; feelings always leak out non-verbally. Distribute Handout F.	10
Body Language and Behaviour Types Exercise Feedback	10
Explain Toolkit. Describe each skill separately, working from the poster. Demonstration of Skills Exercise. Discussion and Distribution of Handout G.	15
Break	15
Explain role-play, using Handout H. Demonstration Role-play Exercise	15
Working in threes, ask people to take turns to role-play the first situation on their personal programme. Facilitator works with each group in turn. Feedback in large group.	30 5
Closing exercise: share with the group something that they have learnt about their body language.	5

BODY SPACE
Respect other's space.
Too close? Too far?

ASSERTIVE STANCE
Stand tall.
Hold your head high.
Feel strong and equal.
Believe in yourself.

FACIAL EXPRESSION
Is your face saying what you are saying?
GESTURES
Avoid fidgeting.
Use appropriate gestures.

EYE CONTACT
Look at the person – not at the ground.
Avoid a fixed stare.
Use a comfortable, direct gaze.

INTONATION
Be interesting not monotonous.
Avoid sarcasm.

VOLUME
Adjust your volume control.
Check your speed.

HANDOUT G *The Toolkit*

Contained in the toolkit are the following assertive skills:

Body language	This skill is explained and illustrated in Handout F.
Setting the scene	This is to help you to feel in control in the situation. Choose the time and place. Clarify what you want to say. Decide what you would like from the situation.
Disclosing feelings	This skill can easily be forgotten; it is, however, extremely effective. Use 'I' statements, own your feelings: eg. 'I feel angry,' 'I feel happy.' Take responsibility for how you feel; avoid blaming others.
Being clear	Assertive communication requires concise, specific speech. Use short, clear statements. Avoid unnecessary padding.
Staying with it	Use this skill in conjunction with empathising. Stay with your statement. Avoid getting hooked or side-tracked.
Empathising	In order to communicate with respect and equality we need to empathise with the other person. Acknowledge that you have heard what the other person has said.
Working for a compromise	This skill enables both parties' needs to be met. Assertiveness is not a matter of winning. Compromise leaves both parties feeling good.
Remember	**You can carry this toolkit with you wherever you go.**

HANDOUT H *Role-play*

There are three key people involved in any role-play.

Person A	**Person B**	**Person C**
The person whose role-play it is.	The person (or persons) with whom A wishes to communicate.	The observer.

What your roles are:

Person A   Briefly explain the situation, then role-play your situation as many times as you want, until you feel happy with it.

Person B   Avoid overplaying or underplaying your role. Avoid suggesting your way of doing things.

Person C   Give helpful constructive feedback on body language and the use of the other assertive skills.

Do not spend too long in discussion — just DO IT!

Remember

Role-play is the most effective way to learn how we can change our behaviour.

SESSION THREE   Exercises

Body Language and Behaviour Types

Explain to the group that each member moves around asking other people to lend them five pounds, in a passive, indirectly aggressive, directly aggressive and assertive manner. Stress that there is no need to reply to the request. The aim of the exercise is to demonstrate the different body language that corresponds with each behaviour: eg. direct aggression — loud, demanding tone of voice, invading others' body space. Feed back in the large group what they noticed about the differences in body language.

Demonstration of Skills

The facilitator chooses one situation as their theme to demonstrate how each skill works: eg. refusing a special offer made by a salesman.
Refer to the text in *Chapter* 3 (Mohammed talking to his doctor) for a clear example of how you could do this.

Demonstration Role-play

The facilitator asks for a volunteer who is prepared to do their role-play in front of the group. This enables people to understand their roles and to see how the facilitation works. Participants then divide into groups of three to do their own role-plays. The facilitator observes one role-play in each small group from start to finish. It may not be possible to observe everyone's role-play in each session, but you should aim to have seen at least one role-play from everyone by the end of the course. The facilitator's role is to encourage participants to take reponsibility for giving feedback and to suggest skills that may be helpful for Person A to use.

Resistance to role-play is natural and something we all experience. Beware of groups spending too long discussing each situation, rather than moving into the role-play. Ensure that you allow enough time for role-play in each session. The really important message to get across to people about role-play is not to talk about it but to DO IT!

SESSION FOUR

Handouts: I   *The Rights Charter*
                J   *Thinking Assertively*
Exercises: Rights Fantasy
                Assertive Thought
                Role-play
Equipment: Flipchart and pens

Content	Time in minutes
Sharing and Feedback	15
Distribute Handout I. Discuss the Rights Charter, explaining its relevance to assertiveness. Work through the list of rights, encouraging participants to discuss their views. Emphasise: assertiveness means standing up for your rights and respecting the rights of others; the rights take time to sink in; guard against becoming too rights-conscious.	15
Rights Fantasy Exercise	10
Break	15
Explain the relevance of Assertive Thought and distribute Handout J.	10
Assertive Thought Exercise	10
Role-play: continue working through personal programmes. Feedback	30 10
Closing exercise: share with the group a right which you have been denying yourself.	5

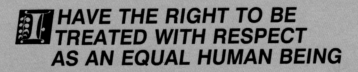

HANDOUT I
The Rights Charter

I HAVE THE RIGHT TO BE TREATED WITH RESPECT AS AN EQUAL HUMAN BEING

I HAVE THE RIGHT TO ACKNOWLEDGE MY NEEDS AS BEING EQUAL TO THOSE OF OTHERS

I HAVE THE RIGHT TO EXPRESS MY OPINIONS, THOUGHTS AND FEELINGS

I HAVE THE RIGHT TO MAKE MISTAKES

I HAVE THE RIGHT TO CHOOSE NOT TO TAKE RESPONSIBILITY FOR OTHER PEOPLE

I HAVE THE RIGHT TO BE ME WITHOUT BEING DEPENDANT ON THE APPROVAL OF OTHERS

HANDOUT J *Thinking Assertively*

This is the art of thinking positively about ourselves and our lives.
Negative thoughts lead to negative behaviour.
Try challenging your self put-downs, changing them instead into positive statements:

Self put-down: 'I'll never be able to do this.'
Challenge: 'I'll have a go, and see how I get on.'

Try to avoid the use of 'imperatives', such as:

I should

I ought

I must

Replace them with words that imply choice:

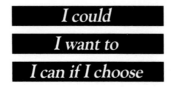

I could

I want to

I can if I choose

Remember

We need to think assertively before we can behave assertively.

SESSION FOUR   Exercises

Rights Fantasy

Ask people to choose one right from the Charter which they find difficult to accept. Suggest that the group relax in their seats and close their eyes. Ask them to think of the right they have chosen, what it means to them and how they feel about having it. After a short silence, tell them to imagine their right is being taken away. Ask them to consider what this loss will mean to them and how they feel about their right being violated. Ask them to decide whether they wish to keep the right for themselves or not. Encourage sharing of experiences in the large group.

This exercise is derived from a more complex rights fantasy, as detailed in *Responsible Assertive Behaviour*, by **Lange and Jakubowski**.

Assertive Thought

Ask the group to brainstorm examples of negative messages they give themselves. Write them on the left-hand side of the flipchart. Point out where participants use imperatives such as 'should', 'must', 'ought', 'have to'. Now ask individuals to suggest positive alternatives to each of their negative messages. Record these in the right-hand column of the flipchart. Encourage discussion on the effect these messages have on our self-esteem.

You may like to consider using one of the following exercises as an alternative to the one listed in the session plan:

Creating Your Own Rights Charter

Divide into small groups, with a large sheet of paper and pens. Ask participants to write their own Rights Charter. Point out that their own rights will usually be personalised versions of the original. For example, 'I have the right to religious freedom' relates to rights one and three. Share these in the large group.

Denying the Rights of Others

Working in pairs, consider the Rights Charter. Select three rights and discuss how you may deny these rights to other people. For example, when we ridicule someone for having an opinion that differs from our own we are denying their right to express their opinions, thoughts and feelings. Feed back to the large group.

SESSION FIVE

Handouts: K   *Owning Our Feelings*
Exercises: What are Feelings?
               Role-play
               Relaxation
Equipment: Flipchart and pens
               Pillows, cushions or mats

Content	Time in minutes
Sharing and Feedback	15
What are Feelings Exercise	10
Discuss the subject of feelings. Emphasise: need to acknowledge them, whether positive or negative; the link between emotional states and physical changes; the risks of denial and repression; how our culture discourages honest expression; feelings leak out non-verbally. Distribute Handout K.	10
Discuss the concept of self-disclosure. Emphasise: the need to self-disclose to reduce anxiety, and the importance of using 'I' statements and not blaming others. Demonstrate this by expressing feelings to the group. Example: 'You make me feel angry when you behave this way,' as opposed to 'I feel angry when you behave this way.' Feed back on the different effects of these statements.	10
Brainstorm ways of physically and cognitively releasing feelings.	5
Break	15
Role-play: continue working through personal programmes, stressing the use of self-disclosure as an assertive skill. Feedback	30 5
Relaxation Exercise Feedback	15
Closing exercise: share with the group something you feel good about.	5

HANDOUT K *Owning Our Feelings*

This involves taking responsibility for acknowledging our feelings and how we act on them.

▶ Feelings are both physical and emotional sensations within our bodies. We can learn to identify what we feel from different body cues, like a lump in the throat or butterflies in the stomach.

▶ It is unhelpful to think of feelings as either 'bad' or 'good', as this can lead us to repress and deny those we consider to be negative.

▶ Disclosing our feelings openly and honestly can enhance the quality of all our relationships.

▶ Avoid blaming others for our feelings: instead of "You make me feel angry", say "I feel angry when . . ." This indicates that we are taking responsibility for the way we feel.

▶ Bottling up our feelings can be destructive. We need to learn ways of physically and mentally releasing them.

Remember

People are not mind-readers — we need to tell them how we feel.

SESSION FIVE   Exercises

What are Feelings?

Ask the group to brainstorm all the feelings they can think of. Record them on the flipchart. Encourage them to continue until it is full. Make the following observations: how there are often more 'negative' feelings than 'positive', and how many different feelings there are.

Relaxation

Ask the group to get into a comfortable position, either sitting or lying. Talk the group through a simple relaxation exercise. Begin with the following breathing exercise.

Tell the group to regulate and calm their breathing by breathing in through their nose and out through their mouth, aiming to take the breath from as low as possible (eg. diaphragmatic breathing). Continue with this pattern of breathing throughout the rest of a simple relaxation exercise. Encourage feedback.

Additional exercises:

Feelings Exercise

Participants sit in a circle with the facilitator, who explains that everyone takes it in turns to say the same phrase, 'I feel sad when . . .' and them complete it with whatever they choose: eg. 'I feel sad when my child hurts himself.'

When the whole group, including the facilitator, has contributed, repeat the process, using the phrase, 'I feel happy when . . .': eg. 'I feel happy when the sun shines.'

Feedback: ask people how they felt in each half of the exercise. What differences did they notice in body language? Were they affected by others' feelings?

Points to make: that it is impossible to disguise our feelings; they will always reveal themselves through our body language.

Relaxation Exercise

This is an example of a simple body scan, which should always be preceded by a breathing exercise. Starting from the feet, work slowly up the body, asking participants to tense and relax each muscle group. Work in the following order: feet, legs, buttocks, stomach, shoulders, arms, hands, neck, head, mouth, eyes and forehead.

You may need to repeat this, asking participants to concentrate on, rather than move, each part of the body. Use relaxing images to encourage mental relaxation. Gently bring the participants back to sense the atmosphere and environment. Suggest that they gently open their eyes and reawaken in their own time. Always provide time for feedback afterwards.

SESSION SIX

Handouts: *L*   *Refusing and Requesting*
Exercises: Saying 'No'
              Asking for what we want
              Role-play
Equipment: Flipchart and pens

Content	Time in minutes
Sharing and Feedback	15
Discuss difficulties of saying 'No'. Emphasise the beliefs — people will think we are selfish; we must always help others; we will hurt their feelings.	10
Saying 'No' Exercise Feedback	15
Discuss difficulties of asking for what we want. Emphasise: dropping hints leads to misunderstanding; there is a risk — we may not always get what we want; asking demonstrates that we value ourselves.	10
Asking for what we want Exercise Feedback	10
Break	15
Role-play: continue working through personal programmes, either saying 'No' or making a request. Feedback	30 10
Closing exercise: share with the group one thing that you would like to ask for.	5

HANDOUT L *Refusing and Requesting*

Refusing Requests

A verbal 'No' with a non-verbal 'Yes' equals confusion: ensure your body language is complementary, rather than contradictory.

How do you know when you want to say 'No'? Listen carefully, check what your body is telling you. Is it a sinking or rising feeling?

Be clear . . .
if in doubt, ask for more time or more information.

Be direct . . .
ensure that you use the word 'No' in the sentence.

Be honest . . .
avoid making long-winded excuses or blaming others; use a simple explanation where appropriate.

Be firm . . .
set limits, recognising them as yours, and that other people's limits will be different.

Be equal . . .
acknowledge the right of the person to be upset by your decision. Be sure to emphasise that it is the request that is being rejected, not the person.

Remember

Saying 'Yes' when you want to say 'No' means short-term gain, but long-term pain.

Making Requests

Being assertive involves taking care of our own needs as well as those of others.
State directly what it is you want or need. Hints and insinuations merely confuse people.

Remember

Take a risk and ask for what you want; it is worth it!

SESSION SIX   Exercises

Saying 'No'

The idea of this exercise is that participants practise using the word 'No'. Point out the need to give a clear message by matching the verbal with the non-verbal. Look out for smiling or head-nodding while saying 'No'.

Ask the group to form two lines, A and B. Line A faces Line B, each person standing opposite a partner. Line A then says 'No' to their partner, who responds with 'Yes'. Continue for several minutes then reverse the roles, Line B saying 'No', Line A 'Yes'.

Feed back the feeling generated by saying 'No'. Did they find it difficult to link the verbal with the non-verbal message? Did they find themselves becoming firmer as the exercise went on?

Ask the group to return to form a circle. Ask each member to consider a reasonable request they could make of their 'neighbour': eg. "Could you lend me your coat until tomorrow?" Each person takes it in turn to make the request; their 'neighbour' replies, saying 'No' while acknowledging their needs: eg. "No, I don't want to lend you my coat, Sally, although I appreciate you want to borrow it." The facilitator starts the exercise by modelling an assertive response to their neighbours' request. By the end of the exercise everyone will have made a request and refused one. Encourage discussion, covering all points mentioned in the session plan.

Asking for what we want

Ask the group to consider individually what they would like to ask for, but never have. Record this on paper and then share in pairs. Feed back in the large group.

SESSION SEVEN

Handouts: M   *Self-Respect*
Exercises: Building Self-Respect
                 Strengths and Weaknesses
                 Giving Compliments
                 Role-play
Equipment: Flipchart, paper and pens

Content	Time in minutes
Sharing and Feedback	15
Discuss the concept of self-respect. Emphasise: raised self-respect is central to assertive behaviour; taking risks can build it; need to accept ourselves as we are; avoid making comparisons. Distribute *Handout* M	10
Building Self-Respect Exercise	10
Strengths and Weaknesses Exercise	10
Introduce the subject of compliments. Emphasise: difficulty of 'letting them in'; importance of not rejecting them; giving and receiving compliments becomes easier as assertiveness increases.	5
Giving Compliments Exercise	10
Break	15
Role-play: continue working through personal programmes.	30
Feedback	10
Closing exercise: ask the group to give a genuine compliment to their 'neighbour'.	5

HANDOUT M *Self-Respect*

▶ Behaving assertively demonstrates that we value ourselves.

▶ Each time we behave assertively our self-respect rises.

▶ Accepting ourselves as we are is more productive than constantly comparing ourselves with other people.

▶ When things go wrong in our lives we need to remind ourselves that we are worthwhile.

▶ Demonstrating respect for ourselves leads to gaining respect from others.

Compliments
▶ Learning to 'let in' the compliments we are given increases our self-esteem.

▶ Accept a compliment gracefully — check that you are not throwing it back in someone's face.

▶ Disclose your positive feelings — give compliments to others.

Remember

Taking the risk of trying something new is a good way of building self-respect.

SESSION SEVEN   Exercises

Building Self-Respect

Ask the group to brainstorm all the ways they know of raising self-respect, and record these on the flipchart. Try also to include ideas that people may not have mentioned: eg. making a scrapbook of cards, letters etc from people whom you care about; listing your positive qualities in the front of your diary so you can read them daily; using assertive thought to challenge self put-downs; finding time to give yourself pleasure every day: eg. having a long soak in the bath. Stress the point about building self-respect being a continuing process and how increased assertiveness can develop it.

Strengths and Weaknesses

This exercise is in itself a method of building self-respect. The aim is to encourage clients to acknowledge both their 'positive' and 'negative' qualities. Ask each member to spend time alone in the group considering six personal strengths and six weaknesses. Suggest they record these to keep. By acknowledging that for every weakness we have a strength, we achieve a balanced view of ourselves.

Giving Compliments

The facilitator demonstrates four different ways of giving a compliment for the benefit of the group. Choose one example to use throughout, such as complimenting someone on their appearance. Demonstrate giving the compliment passively, indirectly, aggressively and assertively. Encourage feedback.

SESSION EIGHT

Handouts: N   *Receiving Criticism*
             O   *Giving Criticism*

Exercises: Valid and Invalid
              Role-play

Equipment: Flipchart, paper and pens

Content	Time in minutes
Sharing and Feedback	15
Discuss difficulties of receiving criticism. Emphasise: criticism starts in childhood when we are vulnerable; crumple-buttons; can be a gift if we learn from it and let it go; brainstorm labels given as children.	10
Distribute and explain Handout N.	10
Valid and Invalid Exercise Feedback	20
Break	15
Outline important points about giving criticism, including: difficulties of doing it constructively; temptation to avoid it altogether or confront aggressively; need to be specific and not personalise criticism; asking for the person's point of view; stating your limits.	10
Distribute Handout O. Role-play: continue working through personal programmes, using situations involving giving criticism.	30
Feedback	5
Closing exercise: share with the group something you value about yourself.	5

HANDOUT N *Receiving Criticism*

Step one   Be sure to listen carefully to what is being said.

Step two   Check that you understand; if not, ask for an example.

Step three Avoid the old conditioned responses:
                Direct Aggression — denying it vehemently
                Indirect Aggression — saying nothing, sulking
                Passivity — believing it is all true

Step four   Decide on the truth of the criticism; is it:
                completely true?
                partly true?
                wholly untrue?

When the criticism is **completely true**:

Say so clearly	"Yes I agree, I am lazy."
Explain how you feel	"I feel bad about it."
Enquire how your behaviour affects others	"Does it make things difficult for you?"

When the criticism is **partly true**:

Agree with the part that is true	"You're right, I can be irresponsible sometimes . . ."
Deny the rest	"But I'm usually a sensible person."

When the criticism is **wholly untrue**:

Reject the criticism firmly	"No, I don't agree, I'm not stupid . . ."
Add a positive personal statement	"I'm an intelligent woman . . ."
Ask why they think this	"What makes you think that?"

Step five   Consider what you have learnt from the criticism. Decide if you want to alter your behaviour as a result.

Remember

Avoid hanging on to it — let it go!

HANDOUT O *Giving Criticism*

This needs to be done constructively.
Avoid making vague insinuations or direct personal attacks.

Step one: Talk positively to yourself, acknowledge that the other person has the right to be treated with respect.

Step two: Choose the time and the place; ensure privacy.

Step three: Avoid vague generalised statements: "This typing's a real mess." Make clear, specific statements instead: "When I checked my letters I found several spelling mistakes."

Step four: Express how you feel: "I feel anxious about discussing this with you; however, when I checked my letters I found . . ."

Step five: At this stage it is important to open up the discussion by asking for the other person's point of view: "Why do you think this is happening?" and how the situation could be resolved: "How can we sort this out?"

Step six: State clearly what the outcome of their new behaviour will be; if you have reached an agreement it will be positive: "I'm sure this will really improve the image of our department." If there is no agreement you will need to spell out what you want to happen and what the negative consequences will be: "I'd like you to check all your letters before they come to me; if there is no improvement in your work by the end of the month, I'll have to discuss it with the personnel department."

Step seven: Summarise the points that you have agreed on, ending with a positive comment.

Remember

Putting off giving criticism only prolongs the agony!

SESSION EIGHT   Exercises

Valid and Invalid

Ask each participant to make a list of approximately ten criticisms which they have received, mixing together the true and the untrue. Divide into pairs and exchange lists. One person practises responding to one of their own criticisms given to them by their partner. Then they offer a criticism to the other person who practises their response. Take it in turns to give and receive criticisms until the lists are finished.

Important: do not allow people to deal with several criticisms in succession, as this can be too difficult for them to take, and lower their self-esteem.

As this is a difficult exercise it can be helpful for the facilitator to demonstrate dealing with one of their own criticisms in front of the group.

Additional Exercises

Letting go of Criticism

Ask participants to draw a criticism they remember receiving. It may be a memory that goes back to childhood, or something which happened last week. Stress that this is not a test of artistic ability, simply a different way of expressing themselves. In commiting what are usually strong feelings to paper, people can become quite emotional and feel unable to share their pictures other than with a partner. However, if it feels right to do so, sharing their experiences with the large group can be very releasing. As each person explains their picture, and the feelings they experienced at the time, it can be helpful to ask 'What would you like to say to that person now?' Their responses are often a way of laying to rest the hurt of the experience, and allowing them to finally let the criticism go.

N.B. This exercise can release very powerful feelings, and so should be treated with respect.

Giving Criticism

Ask participants to think of a criticism they wish to give to someone, and to work out what they might say using the steps described. Suggest they form into pairs or threes to share their 'scripts' with each other. Encourage feedback at the end of the exercise before moving into role-play.

SESSION NINE

Handouts: P   *Sexuality and Sensuality*
Exercises: Sharing Exercise
               Role-play
               Sensual Relaxation
Equipment: Flipchart and pens

Content	Time in minutes
Sharing and Feedback	15
Discuss issues and their link with assertiveness: eg. society's messages, body image, sexism. Ask the group to brainstorm their own ideas of the meaning of sexuality and sensuality. Distribute Handout P.	10
Sharing Exercise and Feedback	25
Break	15
Role-play: continue working through personal programmes. If participants wish, concentrate on a sexual/sensual situation, eg. dealing with a sexist comment or asking for a sensual need to be met.	30
Feedback	5
Sensual Relaxation Exercise	15
Closing exercise: share with the group a sensual pleasure to seek out	5

HANDOUT P *Sexuality and Sensuality*

Society's Messages

These differ for women and men:

Men may feel pressurised to be tough rather than tender, physical rather than emotional. They can be expected to make the first move in a relationship and to be untiring sexual performers.

Women may feel pressurised to be dutiful and willing sexual partners. Initiating in a relationship or asking for their needs to be met can result in being labelled 'cheap'. Refusing to participate in love-making may mean being called 'frigid'.

Body Image

The media exerts strong pressure on both sexes, but especially women, to conform to certain physical stereotypes. The media image of women is one of youthfulness, slenderness and beauty, and suggests that these qualities are all necessary in order to be seen as sexually attractive.

Men are encouraged to appear hunky, strong and muscular in order to display their virility and sexuality.

Sexism

This is so common in our society that we often fail to notice it. Assertiveness encourages us to think and behave as equals, and to challenge sexism, whatever its form.

Sensuality

This means depending on the senses rather than the intellect. Spending time enjoying all our senses, including those we might consider less important, such as touch, taste and smell, can heighten our enjoyment of life. Encouraging those close to us to do the same can be rewarding for all of us.

Remember

There is nothing wrong in identifying a sensual need and meeting it.

SESSION NINE   Exercises

Sharing

Ask the group to divide into pairs or threes. Suggest they allow their discussion to flow around the points raised, based on their own experience. Helpful prompts are: sharing favourite sensual experiences; coping with sexism; the pressures from the media; messages they have received about sex and sexuality. As this is a sensitive topic, it is important to allow the groups to work at their own pace.

Sensual Relaxation

Ask the group to relax comfortably in their chairs and close their eyes. Use a breathing exercise to promote relaxation and then ask them to gently explore their own hands. Direct them to run their fingers slowly and softly over their hands, noticing what touch is pleasurable. Encourage them to explore their palms and fingers, the backs of the hands and nails. Suggest they notice how different touch and movements can create different sensations. Allow participants to continue gently, giving time for silent thoughts. Ask them to think of pleasurable sensations, like the warmth of the sun or the heat of a fire, to promote relaxation further. Towards the end of the exercise you will need to bring their awareness back to the room, before asking them to place their hands in their laps and slowly open their eyes. Allow time for sharing their experience.

SESSION TEN

Handouts: Q   *The Assertive Option*
Exercises: Power Exercise
A Note to Ourselves
Self-Affirmation
Equipment: Flipchart and pens, writing paper and envelopes; drawing materials

Content	Time in minutes
Sharing and Feedback	15
Explain the concept of assertive power by using Handout Q. Emphasise the difference between power and oppression and how we abuse, misuse and give away our power. Brainstorm the meaning of assertive power within.	20
Power Exercise and Feedback	10
Discuss how participants can develop their learning further. Explain what options there are for people to take. Be clear about what you are prepared to offer in the way of support or follow-up work.	10
Break	15
A Note to Ourselves Exercise	10
Self-Affirmation Exercise	30
Closing exercise: share with the group something you are leaving behind, and something you are taking with you.	10

HANDOUT Q *The Assertive Option*

▶ The word **power** is often confused with **oppression**.

▶ Assertiveness involves us becoming aware of our power within.

▶ **Direct aggression** abuses power, by punishing others and denying them their rights.

▶ **Indirect aggression** misuses power, by inducing guilt through emotional blackmail to control other people.

▶ **Passivity** gives away power, by opting for the approval of others.

▶ **The assertive expression of power requires:**

Honesty	rather than	Deceit
Equality	rather than	Injustice
Compromise	rather than	Victory
Sharing feelings	rather than	Hiding feelings
Taking responsibility	rather than	Blaming others
Taking the initiative	rather than	Waiting for rescue

Remember

You can now choose to be assertive.
Act rather than react.

SESSION TEN   Exercises

Power

Ask the group to divide into pairs or threes, to discuss how they use their own personal power. Suggest that they talk about the times when they have abused or misused or have given away power, and consider the results of this. Encourage discussion of times when they have taken the assertive option. Feed back in a large group if necessary.

A Note to Ourselves

Give each participant some notepaper and an envelope. Ask them to write a note to themselves, including what they have learnt on the course and setting themselves three goals that they would like to achieve in the next month.

When they have finished, ask them to seal their envelopes and address them to themselves. They then exchange them with their neighbour, whose responsibility it is to post the letter one month after the end of the course.

Encourage participants to contact the sender to discuss their progress after they have received their letter.

Self-Affirmation

Ask each participant to draw a picture of something they find beautiful. The image can be anything except a person. Tell them to write five qualities that this image has on the drawing. In a round, ask each participant to show their picture and talk about the qualities they have given it. At the end of the round ask participants to speak again, this time owning the qualities for themselves. The idea is that we will project the qualities that we unconsciously see in ourselves onto the picture. Although participants often find this hard to do, encouragement should be given for them to accept the qualities as their own, wherever possible.

APPENDIX II Resources for Facilitators

Training Opportunities in Assertiveness

Stephanie Holland and Clare Ward offer courses in assertiveness for both personal development and clinical application. They can be contacted through the publishers.

Redwood Women's Training Association, 20 North Street, Middleton, Manchester M24 6BD. Telephone 0161–643 1986.
(This association, founded by Anne Dickson, has a network of trainers throughout the country who provide courses in assertiveness.)

Local Adult Education Departments.

Extramural Departments at Universities.

Local Health Education Departments.

Facilitators' Book List

In addition to Handout B, we recommend the following titles:
Bond M, *Being Assertive. Workbook Manual for Nursing Staff*, South Bank Poly Distance Learning Centre, London 1987.
Brandes D and Philips H, *Gamesters' Handbook*, Hutchinson, Newcastle-upon-Tyne, 1977.
Dickson Anne, *A Woman In Your Own Right*, Quartet, London, 1982.
Elkins DP, *Ideas and Activities for Building Self-Esteem*, Growth Association, 1979.
Hewitt J, *The Complete Relaxation Book*, Rider, London, 1986.
Kelley Colleen, *Assertion Training — A Facilitator's Guide*, University Associates, San Diego, California, 1979.
Lange A and Jakubowski P, *Responsible Assertive Behaviour*, Research Press, Illinois, 1976.
Muir Liz, *Assertiveness Skills for Young People*; contact the author, 0161–434 1260.
Rowan J, *Reality Game — A Guide to Humanistic Therapy and Counselling*, Routledge & Kegan Paul, London, 1983.
Townend Anni, *Assertion Training*, FPA Education Unit, London, 1985.
Yalom ID, *The Theory & Practice of Group Psychotherapy*, Basic Books, New York, 1988.

Developing Awareness of Sexuality

For developing further awareness of sexuality, the following opportunities are available which can be discussed with participants.

Training

The Family Planning Association, 2–12 Pentonville Road, London N1 9FP. Telephone 0171–837 5432. The association offers training courses throughout the country which are aimed at a variety of professional groups.

The Redwood Women's Training Association, 20 North Street, Middleton, Manchester M24 6BD. Telephone 0161–643 1986. The association has a network of trainers throughout the country who run group sessions for women on sexuality.

SPOD, 286 Camden Road, London N7 0BJ. Telephone 0171–607 8851. The Association to Aid the Sexual and Personal Relationships of People with a Disability provides an advisory and referral service for disabled clients, therapists, counsellors and educators as well as training courses throughout the country.

Personal Development

Local clinical psychology departments and community mental health teams may offer counselling and group therapy for those with problems in this area.

Suggested Further Reading

Crenshaw, Theresa, *Your Guide to Better Sex*, Exley, Watford, 1984.
Dickson, Anne, *The Mirror Within*, Quartet, London, 1988.
Kitzinger, Sheila, *Woman's Experience of Sex*, Penguin, Harmondsworth, 1987.
Rakusen, Jill, *Our Bodies Ourselves*, Penguin, Harmondsworth, 1987.
Zilbergeld, Bernie, *Men and Sex*, Fontana, London, 1988.

References

Alberti and Emmons, *Your Perfect Right*, Impact, San Luis Obispo, 1970.
Concise Oxford English Dictionary, sixth edition, Oxford University Press, 1976.
Anne Dickson, *A Woman In Your Own Right*, Quartet, London, 1982.
Albert Ellis, *Reason and Emotion in Psychotherapy*, Citadel, New York, 1962.
Arthur J Lange and Patricia Jakubowski, *Responsible Assertive Behaviour*, Research Press, Illinois, 1976.
Natalie Shainess, *Sweet Suffering*, Bobbs Merrill, 1984.

Also available from Speechmark ...

Talkabout
Alex Kelly
Providing practioners with a comprehensive framework for the development of social communication skills, this photocopiable manual can be used with children, adolesecents and adults.

Talkabout Activities
Alex Kelly
Containing 225 group activities, this excellent resource is aimed primarily at people familiar with *Talkabout*, although it can be used by anyone running social skills groups and will complement other social-skills training programmes.

Group Activities for Personal Development
Sheena Duboust & Pamela Knight
This highly practical and easy-to-use title covers specific themes for personal development such as learning to trust, developing self-understanding, non-verbal communication, expressing feelings, assertion training and exploring relationships.

Creative Activities in Groupwork *Series*
This hugely successful series has been devised to provide a rich and diverse source of inspiration to anyone running activity groups. Books in this series covers art, drama, relaxation, music, writing, movement & dance, games and action methods. All activities include step-by-step instructions.

Social Skills Programmes: An Integrated Approach from Early Years to Adolescence
Maureen Aarons & Tessa Gittens
Following on from *Autism*, this new publication contains detailed photocopiable sesson plans for early years, infants, juniors and adolescents.

Writing & Developing Social Stories: Practical Interventions in Autism
Caroline Smith
This practical resource provides an introduction to the theory and practice of writing social stories. In addition, there are examples of successful stories to use as guides, as well as information and photocopiable resources for delivering training on the use of social stories.